A
JOURNEY
INTO
TRUTH

ALSO BY ALEXIS GONZALEZ

A Journey into Truth: The Companion Journal
The Dreamers Journal Pt. I
The Dreamers Journal Pt. II

A JOURNEY INTO TRUTH

Unveiling Life's Secrets for Truth-Seekers

ALEXIS GONZALEZ

Vibrate to Create

Copyright © Alexis Gonzalez, 2021
All rights reserved.
Published by Vibrate to Create
Cover Design: Lynn Andreozzi
Headshot Photography: Marcela DeCuir

Publisher's Note

No parts of this publication may be reproduced, stored in a retrieval system, or transmitted in any form or by any means, electronic, mechanical, photocopying, recording, or otherwise, without the prior written permission of the copyright owner. This book is sold subject to the condition that it shall not, by way of trade or otherwise, be lent, resold, hired out, or otherwise circulated without the publisher's prior consent in any form of binding or cover other than that in which it is published and without a similar condition including this condition being imposed on the subsequent purchaser. Under no circumstances may any part of this book be photocopied for resale.

The advice and strategies found within may not be suitable for every situation. This work is sold with the understanding that neither the author nor the publisher are held responsible for the results accrued from the advice in this book. This book does not replace real therapy. This book is for informational and educational purposes and should not be considered a replacement for therapy or other forms of treatment.

While all attempts have been made to verify the information provided in this publication, neither the author nor the publisher assumes any responsibility for errors, omissions, or contrary interpretations of the subject matter herein. Adherence to all applicable laws and regulations, including international, federal, state, and local governing professional licensing, business practices, advertising, and all other aspects of doing business in the US, Canada, or any other jurisdiction is the sole responsibility of the purchaser or reader. Any perceived slight of any individual or organization is purely unintentional.

Paperback ISBN: 978-1-7377650-1-1
Digital ISBN: 978-1-7377650-2-8
Audiobook ISBN: 978-1-7377650-0-4
Printed in the United States of America
Contact vibratetocreate@gmail.com for more information

"Each night, when I go to sleep, I die.
And the next morning, when I wake up,
I am reborn."

- Mahatma Gandhi

Contents

CHAPTER 1

The Rupture that Revealed Light............................. 1

    The Break-Down................................ 6
    The Break-Through 15

CHAPTER 2

The Journey Toward Emergence 19

    Opening the Door to Truth 22
    Stepping Out of the Cave 24
    Aliens, Hippies, Nudists, and Shrooms 25
    Abraham Hicks Cruise—Alaska 28
    Meeting Esther Hicks 34
    Mediums, Psychics, and Trance 38
    Crystals, Ayahuasca, Shamans, and Peru.. 42
    Ayahuasca: Take Two 53
    Family Constellations and Reiki 56

CHAPTER 3

Everything Happens *For* You 63

    The Tree of "Struggle" 66
    Wabi-Sabi 67
    The Mesmerizing Rose 69
    Kintsugi 71
    Impermanence 74
    The Sun Comes Back 77

CHAPTER 4

The Eternal Process of Evolvement 81

    The Fleeting Present Moment 84
    The Expansive Nature of Reality 85
    Embracing the Unknown 87
    The Boy Who Lost His Horse 92

CHAPTER 5

Strength in Surrender 95

    From Prison to Liberation 97
    Riding the Wave 101
    Bobcat in the Bushes 107

CHAPTER 6

The World Goes Blind 111

    There's a "Log" in my Eye 113
    A Story of Forgiveness 117
    "Punishment" out of Pain: An Experience 119

CHAPTER 7

Perfection is Non-Existent,

Diversity is Constant 125

    The Origin of Judgment 128
    Perfection is Non-Existent 134
    Self-Worth and "Beauty" 135
    Authenticity 138
    Dancing for **Yourself** 140

CHAPTER 8

Giving and Receiving 145

> Open to Receiving: An Experience 151

CHAPTER 9

Live *Because* You Will Die..................................... 155

> Choose for Yourself 157
> One Door Closes for Another to Open 163
> The Man Who Needed a Cow..................... 166
> Purpose 167

CHAPTER 10

The Truth.. 171

Epilogue.. 183

Notes 189

Also by the Author... 193

About the Author... 195

A JOURNEY INTO TRUTH

Introduction

Have you ever seen or read *Eat, Pray, Love*? It's a story of a woman whose life, *seemingly,* falls apart. All she planned to do, and all she ever knew, gets destroyed right before her eyes. In this liminal state, she uproots her whole life and goes on an epic adventure. By learning about her life, the audience interprets the meaning of their own lives for themselves.

That one moment of "break-down" was a transitional one, that would eventually lead her into discovering her soul's *purposed* growth and fulfillment.

There's a reason why stories like these are my favorite ones. I can personally identify with these types of characters in my own life's experience. I, too, experienced pain and suffering that preceded a period of transformation. This hardship led me onto a path of in-depth searching for answers. I had questions like: Why are we here? What is the meaning of life, and is there a purpose to being here? What happens after we die? Can the non-living communicate with the living? Is there such a thing as God?

Like the characters of these kinds of stories, my questions led me on an expedition to find the truth, the meaning of life, and the *secrets of the universe.* Now, I hope to help guide others who are seeking the same answers that I once searched for.

Depression, addiction, a suicide attempt, cancer, and the threat of homelessness, became the catalysts that propelled me onto a brand-new life trajectory.

The close encounters I've had with death and the crumbling of the only world I'd ever known, were the reasons I became motivated to explore the metaphysical world. My search for truth was born from the fear of what was on the other side of physical life.

Since my first "stages of awakening," my life has become solely dedicated to passionately exploring ideas like the nature of reality, the meaning of existence, philosophy, the afterlife, morality, and spirituality.

As of writing this book, it's been almost six years since I leaped into this field. I might even say that I was pushed off a cliff into it by life circumstances.

I recently told someone, "I feel like I went to school for the last six years and got a master's degree in spirituality." I didn't actually. My explorations were purely for self-help, self-healing, and to find answers to my questions. I also found it *wildly* intriguing. I began a quest, like the heroes' quests you hear about in fiction stories. It was a personal odyssey into learning *all things* metaphysical.

It was like stepping onto an unknown path, feeling an intense pull (one you must follow) to keep exploring. Like the feeling of having no choice but to itch an itch.

I delved into the minds and worlds of monks, hippies, spiritualists, Buddhists, shamans, psychedelics, psychics, mediums, Ayurveda, Reiki masters; you name it. I picked their minds apart, searching for "the whole truth."

If you're anything like I was, when I went searching for deeper truths, you'll probably learn about manifestation, the Law of Attraction, creating your reality, and the power of positive thinking. On the opposite spectrum, you could meet spiritual people who dislike positive focus but are drawn to "shadow work." Maybe you'll encounter the paths of trauma healing or Wicca, magic, crystals, and rituals.

Perhaps along your explorations, you'll also learn about plant medicine explorers, otherworldly psychedelic trips or shamans, and energetic forms of healing. You may hear about lucid dreaming, miracle healings, old souls, reincarnation, and out-of-body experiences. The list of religions available out there is even more extensive.

From this shortlist of the spiritual routes one can take, you can see how confusing this path can become. How do you choose *your* path? Are any of them more "right" than the others? Is it even true what they're claiming, or is it all fairytales and delusion? Is there a factual basis behind any claims of metaphysical theories?

I hope to clarify some of those questions in this book for you. My opinions are solely based on my thoughts and experiences. I encourage you to explore on your own, as I did. New discoveries are best found within personal experiences.

I'm excited for you to begin your steps toward growth, awakening, expansion, and hopefully, a love for life—like I've found. I hope you meet even half of the interesting, fun, sometimes weird, and *beautiful* people I've had the pleasure of meeting and becoming friends with.

I will leave you here with a quote before you begin your journey through this book. Socrates once stated:

"The only true wisdom is in

knowing you know nothing."

I will be learning for the rest of my life (and even after this one ends).

-With Love,

Alexis

Chapter 1

The Rupture that Revealed Light

I walk through an alley, surrounded by buildings I've never seen before. The darkness and silence of the night consume the spaces between the buildings, like water flooding rooms of a home. I begin to wander, hearing only rocks crunching together beneath my shoes. Yards away from me, something moves. My eyes squint as I try to figure out what it is.

A dark figure comes creeping toward me. My eyes grow wider as it emerges, and looms close enough for me to unveil its identity. The tiger peers at me, through ravenous eyes, as my innate survival instinct activates.

I run for my life. I know that if I begged for him to spare me my life, he wouldn't be concerned. What am I to him, but a source of sustenance to quench his hunger? I just happened to be the one he set his sights on as his next meal.

I run to each door around me to look for unlocked rooms. I think, "Maybe if I hide well enough, he'll find a new target." One room opens—it's a classroom, also flooded with darkness. I hide under a table. He can smell my fear, and this entices him more. A sense of my imminent doom sinks in. My heart pounds as my hunter enters the room, approaching me.

Just before my death, I'm catapulted back into the ordinary world. I lay in bed, sweating with the fear of a danger that was only a figment of my dream world.

Though waking up was a sweet relief, I felt the dream was communicating something to me. I never had one that was so vivid, terrifying, or lifelike. I concluded that it was telling me, "Whatever you run from will find you."

Growth, expansion, and healing are quite literally a journey where you get pushed to the limit of whatever you think you can handle in your life.

When I was a 19-year-old pizza maker, if someone told me I would be trying psychedelics in other countries, training with psychics, channelers, and healers, in only five years, I would've said to you that you had fallen right off your rocker.

The Rupture that Revealed Light

At that age, I couldn't *fathom* the kind of person I would grow into, the people I would meet, or the types of experiences I would have.

Before I explain, I want to share where I was with this whole "mystical field" before I began exploring it.

I grew up in a family with Christian beliefs that centered, primarily, around fear. After my explorations within the fields of spirituality, I developed a brand new (and personal) appreciation for the teachings of Jesus. No churches or "rules" required.

At around eight years old, I was told:

One day the rapture and judgment day will be coming. There will be horses with crickets for heads. The Devil will come to take the people who did bad things and send them into a life of fire and misery. All the good people who followed God (and his rules of what makes you a good person) will be lifted into the heavens for a life of eternal paradise.

I can distinctly remember the image that popped into my young mind—the lucky and holy men and women floating up into the clouds in beams of light. You know, like the kinds of things you see on TV when people are depicting alien abductions.

This is quite against the laws of nature. In the mind of a child, it doesn't necessarily click that this is preposterous information.

The only thing remotely "spiritual" or "mystical" I encountered growing up was when I was around 13 years old. I sat in the backseat of the car as my mom and her best friend drove by a small home.

It was brightly colored, in yellow and white. A big sign out in the front yard read, "Psychic Readings." They looked at each other and apprehensively (but excitedly) decided they would like to get a reading from this psychic. We walked in, they were directed into a small room, and went inside together while I sat in the waiting room.

When they finished, I heard small snippets as I eavesdropped from the backseat of the car. It all seemed so mysterious to me. They were spooked but thrilled as they tried to understand the messages she gave them.

"I bet she was talking about him when she said that, but how could she know that?"

I sat there, eyes flitting back and forth between them, trying to figure out what just happened. I never did figure it out, by the way.

It is such a stark contrast when I compare that experience to my understanding of these topics, now that I've experienced what I have.

My idea of a psychic was this mysterious, magical (and slightly ominous) woman who had supernatural gifts. She peered into crystal balls, wore a weird headdress, had a cool accent, could see into your future, and could read minds. It was your typical movie psychic. Now I think, sometimes, that I'm the one the "normal" people look at that way.

I promise you; I do not look into crystal balls—or any kinds of balls, really (wink, wink).

When I was growing up, my parents would have bursts of being inspired to go to church. Usually, these were only times in life when things weren't going well. It was like we only needed God for help and forgot about "him" when life was going well. When we had periods of reaching out to this higher being, I didn't get to choose if I wanted to go to church or not. It was an obligation to go. Perhaps this was where my aversion to religious rules and dogmatism began.

My spiritual explorations started in my late teens when my life's circumstances caused me to inquire about reality (and the meaning of life).

Now that you've gotten a taste of what my "spiritual" upbringing was like, let's talk about this idea of the "Dark Night of the Soul." If you've been in the spiritual field for a while, you've probably already heard this spiel. I will briefly explain for those of you just beginning, sitting there with puzzled looks on your faces like, "Whatchoo talkin' bout?"

No, I am not talking about the Batman movie *The Dark Night*,[1] though I wish I were.

The "Dark Night of the Soul," sometimes also called "the death of the ego," is a time of darkness that can happen just before someone's spiritual awakening, or shift in consciousness.

Adversity seems to be the precursor to massive periods of growth in one's life. Think of Steve Harvey, who lived in his car for three years while he dreamed of making it as a comedian.

J.K Rowling experienced depression and suicidal thoughts at her life's lowest point before becoming the best-selling author of the Harry Potter series.

It is this state of hardship that gives rise to the desire for change. Moments of pain can become the catalysts that push people to become better than they were before the chaos.

I don't believe that it's necessary to suffer intensely, to become more conscious, or to grow. However, in my own life, I experienced immense internal suffering just before my life changed.

The Break-Down

Have you heard that story of the man drowning at sea? In his desperation, he pleads for God to save him from drowning. Lifeboats come up to this man, who is struggling to keep himself afloat. The people aboard ask him if he needs saving.

He refuses their help because God is going to save him! He eventually drowns in this sea.

When he goes to Heaven, he asks God, "Why didn't you save me?"

God replies, "I sent you two lifeboats."

I once felt like that man who was drowning and pleading for someone to save me.

Between the ages of 14 to 19, I experienced the darkest cycle of my life. Don't get me wrong; I also experienced many moments of love, joy, and happiness. However, among those joyous moments, behind closed doors, I suffered some of my darkest emotional depths too.

At those ages, I experienced self-harm, depression, suicidal thoughts (and an attempt at it), anxiety, panic attacks, cancer, and prescription drug and alcohol abuse.

I appeared to be like any other "normal" and happy teen. On the surface, many of my peers and some of my family members knew nothing about what was going on. Beyond my happy mask that the world got to see, was also a face of tremendous sadness and pain. There are a few impactful experiences that sank me into my greatest depths of "darkness." I will briefly explain.

When I was 16 years old, I found myself lying on a doctor's table as he prepared his ultrasound machine to investigate my neck.

During that visit, the ultrasound revealed a calcified lump on my thyroid. Upon discovering this, the endocrinologist recommended we remove the thyroid since cancer ran in my family. We scheduled a date, and I would soon be lying on a roll-away bed, getting wheeled into an operating room. After surgery, it seemed like everything went well, until a few days later.

My mom rushed me back to the emergency room when my body went into shock. Every one of my muscles was cramping and twitching. My mouth clenched shut as tears of panic rolled down my face. I can distinctly remember being put into a wheelchair, as I couldn't walk on my own.

Was I going to live like this for the rest of my life? In the middle of a hurricane like that, it's hard to imagine it could get better. In those moments of extreme uncertainty, all thoughts of the past and all dreams for the future get tossed into the air. You become forced to face the present moment in all its chaos.

During the operation, my parathyroid was also inadvertently damaged. This tiny gland is responsible for calcium absorption and production—it makes muscles and nerves function properly. My body was no longer able to process or produce the calcium it needed.

I was a 16-year-old facing her mortality in such a real, raw, and tangible way—really, it would have shaken anyone's world, at any age. I was powerless to that moment and circumstance; we couldn't go back in time to undo the surgery.

I have learned that grief and loss can cause us to contemplate the meaning of life. This awareness of the fleeting nature of life can arise from experiencing things like:

- Losing a loved one,
- Having a sickness or terminal prognosis,
- Losing homes or belongings that once seemed permanent,
- or seeing a traumatic event (like a car crash).

Existential questions arise in moments like these. How important is it to be rich if I cannot take it with me when I leave this world? What is the true meaning of happiness? What am I leaving behind that could benefit generations to come? How do I want people to remember me? Have I done what I desired to do in this world: did I live fearlessly, did I travel when I felt like traveling, did I love fearlessly?

These are all questions we must face when the impermanence of life shows us its not-so-pretty face.

A personal experience with loss can also bring us into the contemplation of our spiritual nature; what lies beyond the physical body? Is there an afterlife? Will I live on once I leave this earth? Is there such a thing as Hell, and if so, was I a good enough person to end up in Heaven?

Now, back to my experience. Following my surgery, I had many follow-up visits with doctors and spent some time in home-schooling. While facing so many life transitions at such a young age, my mental health also suffered.

I started to experience periods of immense sadness, anxiety, and depression. Doctors began prescribing me anti-depressants, sleeping pills, and anti-anxiety medications.

When I'd tell them there were no improvements, the type of medication switched, or the dosage heightened. I felt like a guinea pig, like there was no hope to heal my emotional pain. I was learning to depend on an external pill to cure what I could only heal from the inside.

Emotional pain happens internally and spiritually. Without tools to understand how to heal this kind of pain, numbing, running from, or dissociating from the source of pain in many instances, becomes our only option. These methods of coping can begin, especially in childhood. These are the years when we can be brought into a world that subjects us to trauma and pain that we are powerless to. Mental or emotional escape is simply what many of us learn to do to survive.

At that stage of my life, I found it comforting to know that there was a quick fix. I liked knowing that something could take the pain away without me facing it on my own. That was how it became a coping mechanism I adopted for survival in a world that was frightening.

Shortly after confronting the possibility of losing my physical body, I lost a relationship with my first serious boyfriend. We began dating at the end of middle school when I was about 14 years old.

We parted ways when I was 17 years old. I still didn't have access to healthy coping mechanisms. I dealt with a major bodily organ loss and the "loss" of who I was before the surgery occurred. The break-up was the piece that tore down an already shaky foundation, the "straw that broke the camel's back," if you will.

The Rupture that Revealed Light

The only way I knew how to escape from my grief and pain from this loss, was to commit suicide. In my agony, over the crumbling of the world around me, I impulsively took a multitude of pills.

I sat there, having taken an amount that I thought could end my life. I knew I had made a choice that I couldn't take back. What I wanted was not an end to my life—I wanted an end to my suffering.

What would happen if I were not in the world? Would the world *really* be better off not having me in it? What about my family? What happens after I die? Where do *I* go? These realizations sunk in *after* I took them.

Because of these second thoughts I was having, I admitted to my mom what I did. In her panic, she tried to get me to make myself throw up. I lost consciousness shortly after.

I woke up inside an ambulance, lying on a stretcher hooked up to beeping monitors. While looking at the ceiling of this moving van, instead of feeling panicked, I felt incredibly comforted, serene, and calm—like everything would be okay. I slipped back into unconsciousness after that small return to my body.

The next moment, I woke up inside a strange room in a hospital. I was covered in blankets, lying on a bed, with charcoal on my face. When someone overdoses, doctors can give activated charcoal to the patient to help absorb any drugs or toxins in the body.

Though I physically made it out alive through the overdose, I wasn't yet out of the "night" emotionally or spiritually. This break-up, especially, was like my first steps into a black abyss. I would soon be falling into a downward spiral—and an immense disconnectedness from my authentic self.

I continued to run from pain by abusing prescription medications. It grew increasingly easy to ask doctors for higher, stronger, or different prescriptions. Rarely (if ever) was I told by these doctors, "No, you don't need that—what you need is new resources for healing and emotional help."

Prescription pills like anti-depressants and anti-anxiety medications can be beneficial for others. In my own experience, I found that working through my unprocessed trauma and harnessing the power of my mind led to a massive shift in my state of mind. It was a pivotal shift that no pill ever gave to me. It was also a lasting change that hasn't wavered since the moment I began my self-healing journey.

The moment I decided to be the one in the driver's seat of my emotional healing, was the moment in which true healing began.

Imagine a child who has a security blanket. Every time she must leave it behind in the morning, on her way to school, she experiences agony. She cries and screams as she exits her parents' car, wishing she could keep it with her. Without it, she feels unsafe; she feels like she can't be in the world unless this blanket is next to her.

She goes through her school day, and all she can think about is the next time she'll be able to hold her blanket. It affects her ability to interact with other kids her age. She can't even concentrate on her schoolwork. Suddenly, every facet of this child's life is affected by her need for the safety this blanket supplies.

Life would be much easier, and she would have so much more freedom if she didn't need this blanket in the way that she does.

It can become a slippery slope to cope with pain by medicating (with things like mind-altering substances). It can create both a mental and physical dependency, like the child with the blanket. It's like locking chains to your feet that you carry with you, wherever you go.

My experience was that I *needed* to have these medications to interact with others in everyday life. When I had anxiety or knew I would be going into an anxiety-inducing environment, I would take my pill bottle with me or take a pill beforehand. It was much easier to take medicine than to be forced to face my "demons."

You hear people talk about "rock bottom," but one can *never* fully grasp the experience of another. Pain is subjective; one small situation that sends one person into panic may not affect another.

My world was consumed by what was around me, by who I became up to that point. My relationship was part of who I was, "I am his girlfriend."

My body was part of who I was; that was what I was born into. "I am Alexis, and I have this body." I never planned for the possibility of having it cut short.

I was also the "high-schooler." Then eventually, I would become the "college student."

At each stage of my life, my "I" was defined by my life's circumstances. I was my body, my belongings, my roles, my *things*, that would inevitably end. That was Alexis.

Identification with things, relationships, people, and jobs is what leads to suffering. If "I am this body," then when this body gets old, or when I get sick, identifying with "I am this body" can create pain. The temporary must always come to an end.

Before my life shifted, "my body" and "Alexis" showed themselves to be impermanent. The suffering because of that realization began. All these concepts of "This is me, and these are my things" were ripping at the seams. The whole world was morphing, flipping upside down. In that chaos began the search for "What, or who, am I?"

"What you run from will find you."

Transforming into a new form can sometimes be preceded by being "killed by the tiger." Perhaps this death is only the death of one form of "self."

A flower transforms as it reaches out of darkness into the light of the world to bloom. The chick must crack the egg to fight its way out of its surroundings to become new.

A rocket must battle with the forces of gravity as it propels itself toward the ends of the earth. That is, until it breaks through the atmosphere into effortless floating, peace, and quiet.

Pressure means change, and change means a new form. Many times, right after that moment of breaking out of the atmosphere, we find ourselves floating through the atmosphere into pure serenity and silence.

Sometimes nothing needs to change in the external world. The breakthrough can manifest solely within one's state of mind and consciousness.

The Break-Through

At 19, I found myself in that "liminal state," just before my life's own "new beginning." I was in college and working at a pizza place. It was that "party" phase of my life and the part where the most "escaping" occurred. I had some painful experiences within another relationship and was being threatened to be kicked out of my home.

There I was, a 19-year-old, fearfully packing what I had into boxes. I didn't know where I was going to live. My whole future seemed as if the universe catapulted it into immense uncertainty. I had no grasp on my independence. How was I going to support myself? Where was I going to go? How was I going to feed myself? Would a family member be willing to give me a place to stay?

Right before my "shift" began, I had a moment of breakdown. I sat in the backseat of a car having a panic attack. My friend and her boyfriend were upfront, and as he drove, a feeling of doom came over me. Through tears, I told them, "I feel like I'm going to die!"

This idea seemed so certain to me. It was like a premonition that "I" was about to end or that my life here was going to be cut short. The "knowing" of my imminent death plunged me into a deeply rooted fear.

Now, I believe that feeling was my unconscious knowing, that a shift was about to occur in my life. Indeed, I was about to die, but not a physical death. In the words of an old Zen saying, "When the student is ready, the teacher will appear." That was the case for me.

I felt drawn to a man who sat in front of my English college class. I never spoke to him directly, but he would become the person to introduce me to the ideas and understandings that would change my life.

He presented his final project on the last day of class (a research paper and PowerPoint). It was a presentation about the power of music to heal. He explained the ideas of Albert Einstein, talked about physics, and told us concepts about energy, vibration, and healing. He grabbed his guitar and began to play a song. Each strum rippled chills throughout my body.

A profound calmness overcame me, a kind of peace that I had never experienced before. I was completely present, completely accepting of everything going on in my life, outside of that classroom. All fears about where I was going to live, how I would support myself, everything, seemed unimportant.

Have you ever had a dirty windshield for a while? Over time, you become accustomed to looking at the world through that window—even with its water spots, dirt, and bugs that have unfortunately smashed into it. Then you get a car wash, and suddenly as you drive, the world takes on a new view. I love the feeling of seeing that contrast.

When I heard these spiritual ideas and this man sing, it was like my car windshield cleared. I left that class feeling a lasting and deep-seated peace, which transcended all external factors. It was a type of peace that no substance ever gave me access to— a cellular, soul-quieting moment.

I was like a young girl, with darkness caving in around me, searching ceaselessly for the key to escape my prison. That day, I felt like someone slid a key under the door to allow me to open it.

That night, I went home and began my spiritual search. A tsunami came crashing through my life, destroying, and wiping everything clean, allowing me to start anew.

In one fell swoop, in cold turkey fashion, I stopped taking anti-depressants, anti-anxiety medications, sleeping aids, stopped drinking alcohol, and quit smoking. I haven't touched any of those things since that day.

I don't recommend this to everyone—in fact, I would consult a doctor for more information if you're in that situation yourself (I am not a doctor). Sometimes making a choice like that can be dangerous to someone's health. In my case, I was *determined* to change my life, and I wanted to do it on my own.

I felt like the empty hole in me (that I was trying to fill with substances) was filled. I decided I didn't need or want those band-aids anymore. I wanted to crawl out of the cave now, and to face the things I was running from.

This one 15-20-minute presentation had a massive impact on the rest of my life. It seems now as though it was all destined to happen precisely the way that it did—break-down, hardship, sadness, and all.

On that day, in that college classroom, that one moment was the beginning stages of the birth of a "new" Alexis. That was the day my life as *myself* began. My journey into the worlds of spirituality, the metaphysical world, and my inner world, commenced.

Chapter 2

The Journey Toward Emergence

In philosopher Plato's "Allegory of the Cave," prisoners sit chained together in a dark cave facing the back wall. They see shadows moving because, unbeknownst to them, there is a fire causing the projections of these figures.

To them, these shadows are the only plausible form of reality. It is all they've known since birth. How can anyone know anything other than what they've been exposed to in life?

One prisoner becomes free, sees behind this illusion of a "reality," and makes his way out of the cave. Upon his exit, he enters a whole new world and discovers that the shadows are not reality—they are a *product* of reality. There are real people and real experiences, outside of the cave.

While he enters this new way of perceiving reality, he becomes blind because his eyes are not accustomed to the light.

Once this man has this knowledge, he decides to go back into the cave to let the others know. I imagine he would have said something along the lines of, "Guys, these shadows aren't real, there's something even more real than this, there's *real-life* out there, come look!" They have never seen *his* reality; they have only seen the shadows in the cave. That is *their* reality.

Because the freed prisoner returns to these chained men as a blind man, the others are too afraid to leave the cave. They continue to believe that this cave wall is all there is to life. They are happy never to learn the knowledge this man has unearthed. Is it wrong of them to want to protect their perspective, because in their minds, maybe they might like it better inside the cave?

From the moment a child is born into the world, they begin to form their sense of self. It starts with their relationships with parents, family members, teachers, societal expectations and norms, or cultural backgrounds.

The same seedlings planted in two different environments will form and grow entirely differently because their surroundings affect them. This gives rise to uniqueness and diversity. But within humans, this uniqueness can also give rise to opposition or division between those with conflicting views.

Stepping away from all that one was taught, be it belief systems, religions, cultural patterns, or one's inherited self—can be daunting.

Opening to new viewpoints that may threaten deeply held beliefs can feel like a threat to that person's sense of self. Many would prefer to stay in their cave for safety, familiarity, and comfort.

That presentation in college pushed me to take the first "baby steps" of my journey into the worlds of metaphysics. It was the first time I was exposed to ideas, not on the cave wall of the small world I was born into. I wanted to know things that regular schooling and the people around me, didn't allow me to explore.

I yearned whole-heartedly to discover what happens after we die, primarily because of my encounters with death. I wanted to know if the "dead" were still able to communicate with us here. I tried to understand miracles and healings, and to uncover the giant mystery of this thing that was named "God." It was an in-depth search for the *truth*.

The following experiences I've had while learning about spirituality, are a culmination of only small fragments of the last six years of my life. I first began with personal, ideological learning through books and videos.

Over time, that turned into firsthand experiential learning. I was gathering data from listening to people's stories, while also having my own experiences.

This evolved even further, into putting myself right smack dab in the middle of big "spiritual" experiences (like going to the jungle to try ayahuasca), so that I could discover the *real and raw truth* for myself.

Opening the Door to Truth

The first steps I took on the journey I never planned to take, began online. I would research topics like energy, the Law of Attraction, old souls, psychics, channeling, reincarnation, and past lives. At the beginning of this venture into myself, I also chose to get off social media and stopped taking photos of things I was doing.

As a teen, social media became a source of anxiety for me. My sense of self-worth was derived from how many likes or comments I was getting. Throughout the process I was embarking on, I wanted to dive into myself fully, to cultivate my sense of worthiness. I wanted to live *in the world* and encounter whatever I was meant to come across in real physical life—not through a screen.

In my research, one of the first spiritual teachers I was introduced to, was named Abraham Hicks. Abraham is said to be a non-physical entity that speaks through a woman named Esther Hicks. This is called channeling (by some).

When I discovered Esther and Abraham, I felt incredibly drawn to the teachings. I would spend hours each day listening to them on YouTube and began looking into their books. That was where my thirst for more knowledge on these subjects began.

I gathered enough courage to walk into used bookstores. I would quietly (and ashamedly) tiptoe over to the "metaphysical" section. I'd look puzzledly at these "out there" books, while peering around to see if anyone was silently judging me. Funny, how you're reading a book I wrote that belongs in that section, huh?

That first trip to the bookstore, I picked anything in that section that caught my eye, covered the titles (so the other customers didn't know what I was buying), and approached the counter.

It was like that stereotypical (and humorous) depiction of a dad sneaking into a store. He's wandering, trying to figure out where to find tampons and what kind to buy for his daughter's first period. That was me, except I was picking up books about dead people and sixth senses.

That first time buying metaphysical books in public, I handed the librarian multiple books on topics, like Edgar Cayce, psychism, channeling, and the afterlife.

With her silvery hair in a bun, the woman had a look at the books I just plopped down. She peeked over her glasses to look at me and sweetly said, "Oh, Edgar Cayce, that's an interesting one."

I smiled and said, "Yeah," as I prayed internally, hoping she knew I was a sane and "rational" person.

I would take these books with me to parks, coffee shops, and libraries. They would even go with me to school so that I could read them in between my college classes.

These explorations through books from used bookstores and libraries continued for some time. As I became more comfortable with this new world, I looked for free spiritual meetups or churches around me.

I wanted now to learn from people in person. I was dipping my toes into the waters of the diverse world of spiritual teachings this world had to offer me. I like to say this was the stage that I stepped out of the "secret cave."

Stepping Out of the Cave

I began my "in the world" explorations with the Soka Gakkai International Buddhists. I found them through the vast array of free meetups posted online. I heard of Buddhism but never met a Buddhist or learned about what they believed.

They taught me chanting, their beliefs of the afterlife, and their thoughts of our purpose on this earth. They took me in (from the moment they met me) with open arms—like family.

Periodically, they would ask me to help facilitate meetings. I would stand in front of the crowd of 20-30 people to present, read from a piece of paper, and announce the people who would be speaking next.

I loved to learn about this religion's ideas of the afterlife, but my explorations in the world of spirituality never ceased. I wanted to learn *all* opinions and beliefs. I wanted to know the meaning of life for myself, not be told what it was by one group of people. I wanted to know why we were put here, and who put us here. I couldn't stop at one opinion.

To continue learning and to meet people who believed what I believed, I went to free Abraham Hicks meetup groups. We discussed the teachings and books, made vision boards, and shared how the teachings affected our lives.

Around this time, I also began going to meditations with monks and learned basics from an Ayurvedic teacher. Until eventually, I went to weekend-long spiritual festivals alone.

I met and became friends with the "hippie" spiritualists and plant medicine experimenters. Yes, I mean San Pedro, Ayahuasca, and "magic" mushrooms.

Aliens, Hippies, Nudists, and Shrooms

This world opened the door to a whole new path of discovery. I was introduced to my first spiritual festival by an English college professor. After I wrote a research paper on lucid dreaming, she told me about it.

I had no idea what I would be encountering, nor could I fathom who I would meet. Was I going to be sitting in a corner as people walked past me, whispering to their friends, "That's the one weird girl who came by herself"? Oh, the horrors of someone else's opinion!

Sometimes when I tell people I've gone to festivals alone, I'm met with a look of horror, or I'm told, "Oh, no, I could never do that; you're so brave!" I was terrified.

I packed my backpack for my three-day trip, gathered a small one-person tent, went to the store to pick up food for the weekend, and prayed to the ethers that I would make it through the next three days (alive, preferably). It felt like I was walking blindly through the dark, holding a stranger's hand, hoping they were going to lead me to a safe place.

I met a wide range of people who told me they talked to aliens, had lived (or came from) Atlantis, could speak to crystals (or plants, animals, and trees), spoke to the galactic councils, hailed from the Lyrans, used the "violet flame" for healing, could cleanse my chakras—and see my aura. I remember sitting next to a girl in one of the workshops who had hairy legs and armpits, and I thought to myself, "I love this place."

I loved being around so many people who unapologetically said things that would either make a "normal" person run the other way, or make them think that you had lost your mind. That, to me, was fearless authenticity, and I wanted to hear it *all*.

I sat in workshops and had beautiful conversations with strangers. That whole weekend, I listened wondrously to each person like a child hearing a bedtime story. I would say (with twinkling eyes), "Really, tell me some more."

One of my most vivid memories happened during one of the workshops. The workshop leader exclaimed, "I want us all to close with a cinnamon bun hug."

In my head, I thought to myself, "You want to do what now?"

He explained how to do it; we all gathered hands and wrapped around in a circle, one by one, to create a swirl (like a cinnamon bun). So, there I was, standing in the middle of a human cinnamon bun, looking around at the faces of people I knew nothing about. Yet somehow, I felt, "This is the most beautiful experience I've ever had."

That weekend I learned about holistic health. I walked past a nudist workshop (No, I did not join, I was not THAT fearless). I made dreamcatchers and danced around a fire while people played drums. We talked about our most vulnerable selves. We shared hardships we'd been through in our lifetime and were given a safe place to be held in that emotion.

I also learned about essential oil therapy, "Gaia," experienced my first sound bath, and listened to people's life experiences. I ate, laughed, and cried with strangers.

Aside from these experiences, my explorations were ceaseless. After this festival, I continued going to various sound healings, learned about, and experienced breathwork meditations. I went to a sound bath at the "Integratron." I met yogis at a Hindu Holi color festival, joined their small studio, and did Yoga with them for some time. I learned about Kundalini Yoga, different forms of meditation, Slow-Flow Yoga, Aerial Yoga, and Tribal Belly Dancing. Yes, I used the jingling skirt and everything; no, I did not look as graceful as Shakira, I am sad to report. I did feel like Shakira though.

Over the past couple of years, I've probably heard just about every weird, crazy, or different idea that you could imagine. At the beginning of my journey—I could've never predicted that I would eventually take solo trips to spiritual festivals.

These short solo trips would eventually lead to an opportunity for me to travel to Alaska alone. Once I arrived there, it seemed like all those smaller steps, adventures, and previous trips, were preparing me to end up taking even more significant leaps of faith.

Abraham Hicks Cruise—Alaska

In 2017, For my 21st birthday, I was gifted an Abraham Hicks cruise by a family member. They knew how much

I loved to listen to the teachings and wanted to gift me something they knew would change my life.

Seeing a live workshop was a massive dream of mine. When this dream was made manifest, the excitement I felt about it was palpable. It was a cruise to Alaska and Canada. I was about to be sitting in front of this teacher, surrounded by hundreds and hundreds of other people who believed what I believed.

My birthday was in May, and this cruise would be happening in July (it was usually sold out). Someone canceled their reservation last minute—and it made room for me to be on that ship.

As you guys learned earlier in the chapter, Esther and Abraham were some of the first teachers that I encountered on my "healing journey." I'm sure you can imagine my extreme excitement for the opportunity to sit in front of one of the teachers who saved my life. This trip revealed just how much the unknown could be both *terrifying*, and incredibly exciting, all at once.

This was my first time being on a plane; I never traveled that far from home and had never been on a ship. Life, again, put me into another experience where immense trust (that things would work out) was required, vital even.

I felt like a lost child walking through the airport. I stood there, looking around for signs that would point me to where I should pick up my bags as people walked swiftly past me.

Then, I gave up on "looking for signs." I decided the next best way to figure things out was to ask the security guards to find my luggage. They would tell me where, and in my panic, I'd forget where they pointed to and asked someone else.

I held my breath as I tried to piece together the next step of how in the world I could get my body, my luggage, and my sanity (preferably) onto that ship in one piece. I'm happy to report that I did make it there alive, luggage and all.

Those moments have turned out to be my most significant moments of growth. In those moments, I have no choice but to surrender to the unknown, follow my gut, trust, go with the current, and hope I land on safe ground.

Have you ever seen the opening to the movie *Titanic*? Jack Dawson is a poor man who, by chance, wins a ticket to get onto a ship that will be departing five minutes before he wins this ticket. Within minutes he must get to the ship's door (or they will leave without him). It was a life-changing, panicked, and in-the-moment search to get on the ship.

That's how I felt, as I cluelessly asked people around me how to get to my destination in time for the ship not to leave me behind. However, I was thankfully getting onto a ship that was not going to sink (whew).

This cruise was one of the most soul-fulfilling, joyous, and ecstatic experiences I've ever had. I met beautiful people and had many deep conversations with those momentary friends whose faces I'd never see again. I ate a plethora of delicious food (I do not regret even one bite I took).

I looked (with eyes of wonder) at massive glaciers and mountains covered in pure nature. I danced in the middle of a dance floor shamelessly (BY MYSELF)—the kind of dancing you would *exclusively* reserve to your room while you are there alone, and nobody is watching you.

I peered through windows surrounded by an expansive ocean. Occasionally, I was witness to a whale's tail breaking through the surface as if to say, "Hello, welcome!" I fully drank up every moment that those seven days could offer to me.

It's times like those that have taught me the meaning of life. I enjoyed each moment to its fullest capacity and became as satiated as I thought I could ever become. And then, every moment after that, topped itself.

Just when you think it couldn't get better, the world knocks you over with something *even* better. It's as if in those moments, the universe says to you, "Really? Did you like that? Look at this!"

Before attending my first live Abraham Hicks workshop, I cried tearful streams of joy. I was in my room alone, getting ready for the seminar, when a profound love overcame me. It was like I knew that my whole life was about to change; something was about to shift. I headed down to the auditorium, and once the doors opened, I walked to the front row and took my seat. The "Joy is the Key" song played, as I sat, watching the countdown on the projector.

"Three, two, one," and then she walked out—everyone stood up, and I could not stand, I could not move, I felt paralyzed.

You know, in movies, that dramatic moment when a character gets punched and can't hear anything, as everything around them slows down? That's sort of what this moment was like. The world slowed down as everyone else stood up.

I heard in my head something like, "You don't need to stand; she isn't more important than you—we're just as happy to see you here as her." I felt that these were my spirit guides or some non-physical entity communicating with me internally or intuitively. After some training in psychism, I now know that my experience was a clairaudient one.

The only movement I could manage to make was to push my upper body over to bow in my seat. I sobbed aloud between my legs and felt as if I wanted to take my physical body off. It was blocking me from experiencing all the love that I could be experiencing in that moment.

When I tell you it felt like rapturous, pure, and unconditional love flowing into me, that's *such* an understatement. I felt like telling God, "Just take me now, my life's complete, and I would be happy to die right here in this chair." It was like I came as close to knowing God as a human could experience in their lifetime. It was a moment of being encapsulated by infinity, held by the purest love of all.

When she began talking, I could no longer understand English; it seemed like she was speaking gibberish. I don't know what happened (maybe I was having a stroke, maybe it was enlightenment, perhaps an out-of-body experience, who knows). I was eventually able to refocus on her words to understand what she was saying. It was like I was forcing myself back into my body.

I cried for that whole two-hour workshop—and felt *so much* love. The words she said didn't even matter to me. During a workshop break, the woman sitting next to me looked at me kindly and said, "You must be so grateful to be here."

I said through tears, "I've never felt anything like it. That's not human," as I pointed towards Esther. I did not mean that Esther was an alien standing up on the stage. What I meant was that whatever I was experiencing felt like the love of God. It was an otherworldly, supernatural, and *absolutely* pure love.

If you overload a socket with too many volts, it can cause a fire or a malfunction. The socket can only take in so much energy before its system is overloaded. Let's say the energetic frequency of God (or the spirit world) is a pure, unconditional, and unresisted love—the highest frequency possible.

If that energy touches a human—it can feel like a lightning bolt to the system. My take on it is that it takes a much denser form of energy to be inside a human body, than that of the non-physical.

One person, compared to infinity: all things, all people, all places, all of existence—the two are vastly incomparable. I feel that I was experiencing the vastness of spirit compared to *me*. It was like my human form was momentarily experiencing the purest frequency of love possible.

Meeting Esther Hicks

Another experience from this Alaskan cruise that I want to share briefly was when I met Esther Hicks.

On the day of the second to last workshop, at the end of it, I had the idea to give someone from Esther's team my journal. In this journal, I wrote down my experiences while on the ship and why I was so grateful for her (and the teachings). I wanted her to know just how thankful I was. Those past few days were some of the best I'd ever experienced.

Another leap of faith—I was terrified to walk up to the workers to ask if that was allowed. I asked one person from the team, and he told me I should ask Tracy, Esther's daughter, who was sitting next to him. Shaking in my boots again, I asked Tracy, "Hello, can you please give this to Esther?" She said yes and took it.

The next day was our last workshop in the morning; then, we would arrive in Canada. I booked an excursion to visit the Butchart Gardens.

Upon arriving in Canada, other Abraham Hicks group members and I exited the ship, walked across the Canadian border, and were loaded onto buses to get to the gardens. Our guide told us how much time we had to explore the gardens when we got there. Then we were all sent on our way.

I walked along the paths of this garden, took pictures, enjoyed the sights, the hummingbirds, and the fountains. A feeling of discomfort began to consume me. I felt pulled to keep walking in a specific direction, as if by a magnet. It was like something was pushing me, and I couldn't interpret why it was leading me that way.

As I walked, I came across a man from Barcelona that I met the night before, at dinner. When I saw him, I shouted, "Hello!"

He had a look of such *excitement* on his face as he exclaimed, "Esther's right there!" He pointed over to a few yards away from us. I left him and his friends standing there out of my sheer excitement. My feet felt like I was walking on air, like I could not walk fast enough.

I approached her and yelled, "Esther!"

She politely walked closer to me, and I said, "You have my book!"

She looked at me and tilted her head to the side with a look of confusion. So, I clarified, "My journal!"

"Oh, I didn't read it yet!"

"Oh, it's okay."

I thought to myself, "She's a busy woman; she just didn't have time yet." Then, silence.

I looked around, and it sunk in—everyone was staring at me. I was *that* crazy fan, or at least I felt that way. I did not assess the situation before approaching.

I hadn't realized that so many people were there with her. I froze out of sheer terror. There I was, standing in front of the woman who changed my life, and I don't know what the heck to say next. She broke the silence and interrupted my fright-fest by saying playfully, "Well do you want it back?"

I looked away for a moment. There I was, computing in my mind, "Do I, or do I not? That is the question here." At a certain level, I did want it back. I accidentally left some scenic polaroid photos of Alaska in the journal's back pocket, which I couldn't replicate. Then, I began thinking about just how excited I was that she was going to be reading *my* experiences. She was going to know how big of an impact she made on my life.

This moment went from sheer panic to absolute and utter *pure* love. It felt as if my head opened, and water came pouring into my whole body. It was a visceral feeling of every cell of my body filling with liquid love, beginning at my head and falling towards my feet.

The whole world felt like it slipped away, and it was only her and me standing there. It was a moment of complete presence, absolute joy. I looked her in the eyes, and like the world's most excited child, told her, "No, no, no! I want you to *reeead* it."

She giggled and said, "Okay!"

That was all I needed. I felt complete. So, I told her, "But it was very nice to meet you."

"It was nice meeting you too."

For a second, I thought to myself, "Maybe I should get a picture with her." Then I thought, "No, that was enough. I don't need a physical memory of this." I turned around and walked away. That was it.

These moments of experiencing profound states of consciousness, are like moments in time where the reality as you know it gets ripped in two, and you get to step through the tiny crack that opened for you. I don't understand why they happen, and I don't try to replicate them (I don't think I could if I wanted to). However, I am massively grateful to have experienced it within my lifetime.

When I got home from that life-changing trip, my explorations in the spiritual realm, still continued.

Mediums, Psychics, and Trance

Throughout my spiritual searching, I also ventured into the "mystical" side of spirituality, where I had my first tarot card reading. I began taking classes at metaphysical shops on topics like "meet your animal spirit guide meditation" (I found out my animal spirit guide is a squirrel, just FYI).

Around the middle of 2018, I was invited by an Abraham Hicks group member to my first ever platform mediumship demonstration. This was that group I talked about previously, that I found online. We had an online community and met up in person periodically.

Cindy Kaza would be the one demonstrating on the night that they invited me. I didn't know much about mediums. Once I began learning about it, I found it intriguing. After reading about her, I decided I'd like to attend.

I knew about metaphysics, spirits, and the supernatural through my studies and research in the years leading up to that moment. Subsequently, watching a medium up on a stage, giving evidence of life after death, was an exciting opportunity.

When I was researching who she was, that was also the first time I'd ever heard of the "Arthur Findlay College." I found out that this was a school in England, which helped to train professional psychics and mediums.

I watched her with amazement and curiosity on the night of her demonstration. I never once, thought that I would be diving into learning about that area of spirituality with full force just a few months later.

Months later, in this same Abraham Hicks group, somebody posted in the online community about classes with a psychic and medium named Michael Mayo. I spent about two years training with him. He became my first in-person psychic, mediumship, and trance teacher.

Before meeting Michael, I studied books that talked about connections to and evidence of the spirit world by authors like James Van Praagh, Edgar Cayce, Jane Roberts, and Esther Hicks (among many others).

I also had experience exploring my connection to my spirit guides. I used this connection to the spirit world to help me make decisions within my own life. Some may call this voice "intuition," "a gut feeling," or perhaps "angels."

An excellent example of following this guidance happened years ago, when I adopted my dog. The night before meeting him, I jokingly told my brother, "I want to adopt a dog; maybe we should go adopt one, bring him home, and once mom meets him, she won't make us take him back. She'll have to let us keep him." I made a sneaky plan to carry out this operation.

The following day, my mom said (not knowing the joke I told the night before), "Do you guys want to go adopt a dog today?"

We went to several animal pounds, and at almost every cage, she exclaimed, "This is the one, let's get this one!"

My guides were clairaudiently telling me, "No, wait, these are not the ones." I stubbornly held onto this intuitive hit. Hours later, after visiting several pounds, we came across a 7-year-old Black Labrador. He was quiet and timid among the other dogs in his same cage.

We asked to bring him out to meet him. The sun was seeping through the clouds of that rainy November day, and as he sat on the grass, I knelt to meet him face to face.

He put his nose to my nose, and I heard clairaudiently, "This is the one." It was a dead-on, knowing that I didn't need to look any longer.

We adopted him, and he was the perfect fit for our family. He was already potty trained, never chased our cat, was friendly with everyone, never barked, didn't jump on people, and had excellent manners. He was (and still is) a source of easy, unwavering, unconditional love within our family. He was what I was looking for, a *perfect* fit.

This is just one of the many times I have followed guidance that led me to something much better than I could have planned on my own.

When I began Michael's classes, these were helpful towards directing my connection to the spirit world outwardly, to give messages to others. It was helpful to learn through trial and error with others sitting in front of me.

Within that period of learning, I explored deepening my connection to my "guides," the nature of the spirit world, and "sitting in the power."

Sitting in the power, is a way to describe "sitting" with a quiet mind. It is a time in which you move into a silent space, feel into your spiritual power, attune to, and blend with the power of the spirit world. This also helps heighten sensitivities. It is an integral method of development towards helping the psychic or mediumistic reader become more aware of when they are receiving communication, and when it is their own mind speaking.

During classes, I sat for readings and practiced giving them to others. I fine-tuned my sensitivities to changes in the energy of a person or a room. I learned about translating messages from the spirit world in such a way that could help others. I also learned about ethics as a reader, and the responsibility one has, to be principled within that line of work.

It was fascinating to see how accurately I could pick up on what was going on in the "energy" of a room. The most valuable part of this segment of my development was getting feedback on what I was experiencing from other sitters. It confirmed the realness of my experience, and that was extremely exciting.

I learned about trance and trained alongside many other psychics and mediums who had been in the field for many years. I took a workshop with Michael's teacher (Gordon Smith) and watched medium Eileen Davies do a platform mediumship demonstration.

Witnessing people bringing through evidence of life after death still amazes me to this day—no matter how long I've been in this field of metaphysics.

Currently, I don't feel called to work as a medium or psychic reader at this stage of my life. However, life changes all the time—never say never. These experiences taught me how much healing these professions could offer to those grieving a loss. It also taught me how *real* the spirit world is. Aside from me diving into training within those fields, some other life-changing "manifestations" began during that time, as well.

Crystals, Ayahuasca, Shamans, and Peru

At the end of 2018, I attended a spiritual festival, where I met a woman who would come to teach me many lessons about philanthropy, independence, and owning a heart-centered business (among many other subjects).

During this moment of my life, I worked as a background actress and pet-sitter for work. It was not always steady or consistent work, so I wanted to find more reliable work. I loved working as an extra or background actress, as it taught me much about being in front of a camera. I witnessed many exciting moments, and I met people who had huge dreams for their futures.

Watching T.V. personalities give motivational speeches, and seeing firsthand, what life could offer to people who came from difficult or rough circumstances, was immensely inspiring. Being in the presence of many wealthy people also showed me the value of true happiness, apart from material success.

Although it was fun, my passion was not to become an actress. I knew I wanted to teach about what I learned and be of service to others in some way. I was merely working at that job because it was enjoyable and a fun source of income.

Up until that point, I hadn't learned much about crystals. I heard about them, but never felt like I wanted to work with them or use them for healing. At this festival I mentioned, I attended a sound meditation. During this quiet mind-space, I received a clear desire to go and buy my first crystal. Another "intuitive" hit, you could say.

I've learned not to question why I feel like doing something specific. If I think it is the right next step to take, I listen, and I follow it even if I don't know why I'm being inspired to go that way.

I left the meditation and walked over towards the booths to follow this inner guidance. There was a lineup of many of them, but I knew exactly which one I wanted to buy from. I went to the one that caught my eye, picked out a pendant I liked, and said to the woman working there, "Hello, how much is this one, and what is it for?"

She let me know how much it was and began talking to me about crystals. The conversation led to her explaining to me that she was a Kambo practitioner—the Amazonian frog medicine applied through burns in the skin. It causes a wide range of purgatory effects to cleanse the body of toxins.

The secretion that this frog emits, gets placed onto openings (or gateways) of the client's skin. The medicine makes its way into the body through this application process and cleanses it of toxins with its various antibacterial properties and natural chemicals.

She also told me of the retreats in the jungle that she offered. These included Ayahuasca ceremonies with shamans from the Shipibo tribe. At that time, I hadn't yet heard of Ayahuasca, nor did I desire to try it.

She also told me about how she was opening a small booth at a specific mall in one week. She didn't have anyone to work for her yet, since it all happened so quickly. It was a mall extremely close to my home, so I told her, "Oh, I can do it!" I was already wanting to find a steadier job, so this was a perfect opportunity.

That was the day that I began working at a metaphysical shop. During the year I worked there, I learned about running a small business, crystals, and various medicines from the jungle (including Kambo, Ayahuasca, Dragon's blood, and Copaiba oil).

This job also allowed me to continue learning about others' spiritual beliefs and experiences. Each day I would have intriguing conversations about spirituality, psychedelics, and religion, with a wide variety of people (from many backgrounds and of all ages).

When the business owner would stop by, she would tell me stories of her adventures in the jungle, and what she experienced during Ayahuasca. She made everyone she talked to feel like they were her family members. I would watch her with admiration when I was there to witness her interact with customers.

With her, I tried Kambo a few times, went on a retreat deep into the jungles of Peru, met traditional shamans, did Ayahuasca with them twice, went to and marveled at the ruins of Machu Picchu, and I met people from the Matses and Shipibo tribes.

Ayahuasca, a drinkable brew that contains DMT, is said to cause a wide range of effects (including visions, spiritual revelations, and physical purging). Shamans have used it for thousands of years as part of a ceremony to help with physical or spiritual ailments and to help them connect with the spirit world for guidance. Much can be said about this plant medicine—I am not an expert, just someone who took it twice.

Before leaving on my trip to Peru to try Ayahuasca, I met with my dad for lunch. I told him what I was going to be doing—meeting shamans, going to Machu Picchu, trying Ayahuasca, and all. He looked me in the eyes seriously, with concern, and asked, "Is there anything I can say to make you not go?"

"No," I said with certainty.

Despite the fears of others surrounding me, I got onto that plane and headed into the unknown once again. My eyes were closed (figuratively), and I was following my intuition blindly, again.

I would soon find myself in the jungles of Peru, ready for my first true Ayahuasca experience. A few days before our ceremony, we walked through the jungle for what felt like an hour, to get to a healing center.

On the first night, we helped to prepare the Ayahuasca brew. We broke up the tree branches and created a large pile of these strands. These would then go into a large pot to boil with another plant called "Chacruna."

We experienced a "flower bath" facilitated by a shaman on the second evening at this center. She would be guiding us through our ceremony with her daughter. A "Maloca" is a traditional ceremonial hut where ayahuasca ceremonies are held. Typically, the ceremonies are held at night, as ours was.

Before ceremony, we took our places inside the Maloca, sat on our mats, in a circle, and told the group our intentions. I said, "I want to learn how to trust others and to heal any wounds from my childhood that need healing."

The shamans said a prayer, and we each, one by one, walked up to take our first drink. We laid back down in the darkness of the night, and each of us went on our own "healing" journey.

The Journey Toward Emergence

As Ayahuasca began to seep into my body, the shamans began singing Icaros. This is the name of the healing songs that shamans sing during a medicine journey.

I began seeing images of fractals in my mind—it was like looking into a colorful kaleidoscope with constantly changing forms. My hands started to move over my body like they were *being* moved (not by me). It was like moving energy around, within my body. It seemed like I was gathering stuck energy and pushing it up and out through my mouth.

When my hands would reach up towards my mouth, I would yawn. This is said to be a form of purging stuck energy. I also threw up, another form of purging—it felt like emotions were also coming out and into the bucket.

As time passed, the man sitting next to me got up and moved around in the darkness. I started to hear noises and got afraid that he was taking my bucket, that I might need to purge in. I felt a hand touch my stomach—I panicked and yelled, "What are you doing?"

"I felt like you might need a hug."

"No, don't touch me!"

I felt livid. I was so angry that he touched me without asking me first, invaded my personal space, and interrupted the beautiful moment I was having. He popped my lovely bubble! He apologized as he sat back down.

I heard him bowing to me to apologize sincerely, but all I could feel inside was animosity. No part of me had access to a feeling of forgiveness; I was thrust directly and entirely, into my experience of anger.

As he sat back down, I tried to get back into my "happy place." I couldn't push away my anger. Ayahuasca wanted me to look at and experience it. The more I tried to "paint pretty butterflies" over the anger, the worse I felt. This experience revealed to me much of the patterns I have learned within my life (relevant to anger).

I stayed with this anger for a second. I didn't try to change it; I just let myself be angry. I let myself feel as though I had a right to my emotion. When I allowed this anger to be, I felt a shift happen. It then turned into compassion for this man and the experiences which led to him becoming who he was. I now had a deep-seated love for someone who, one moment prior, I hated.

I went back into my inner process and had a deep knowing that I wanted to take another drink of the medicine (if they offered it to us). Shortly after that thought, coming from the darkness of the room, I heard the words, "Does anyone want to take a second drink?" A drawn-out pause of quiet seeped into the moment.

Having already decided before they asked, I replied, "I do." My voice was the only one that answered.

I stood up, not knowing how off-balance I was until I needed to stand. I made it over to the shaman and took my second drink. I laid back down and continued listening to the Icaros being sung. I remember feeling, "This is going to be good! It's going to be beautiful!" Boy, was I in for it.

As this second drink permeated my body, I began to feel an unbearable sense of fear. The Icaros that previously sounded so beautiful, were now dark and scary. I felt like a little girl locked in a dark room, screaming for help.

I begged for someone to turn on a flashlight and panicked whenever someone would turn it off. A feeling of utter, impending doom began to engulf me. I was being swallowed by the blackness, fighting with my own (spiritual) death. I was stuck in my mental prison, with nowhere to run.

It's strange how sometimes the thing you run from the most, is the thing that has the most power over you. It sounds like the tiger from my dream, right?

I yelled and cried out for help. I needed someone to talk me through my pain. I called out to the woman who brought us to the jungle—I needed to "come back to earth." I needed her to assure me that it would soon be over. I told her, "This is not easy!"

"Healing is not always easy."

She walked me through what felt like an eternity from that state of consciousness. The experience was probably only 45 minutes to an hour (I'm guessing here).

During this freak-out, I became sensitive to all sounds around me; it was like I had a sensory overload, with too much information coming at me. The sounds of the jungle, the Icaros, the people around me, everything, seemed to be caving in on me intrusively.

Imagine being in a state of mind where you are experiencing the worst pain of your life. You have no concept of time, no grasp on the fact that this will be temporary and will pass in just a few hours; you feel trapped in this hell.

In my normal state of mind, I'd say, "Oh, I would talk myself into feeling better; I could make it through that." Once taking Ayahuasca, it's like you lose control of your capacity to reason, and you get thrust into the emotion. There is only facing, head-on, that which your typical psyche would push away.

It felt like I had a subconscious box within me. It was an area full of suppressed emotions and past traumas that opened to be released (all at once). One of my teachers uses an analogy of a dirty kitchen. She says, "When your kitchen is dirty, you have to go inside of the kitchen to clean it. You have to be willing to get inside of the messy places if you want to heal."

In this ceremony, I was trying to think my way into feeling better. I can see now that this is a coping mechanism that developed for survival. It manifested so that I didn't have to "enter" the kitchen. Ayahuasca was forcing me to enter the kitchen to look at the mess I had been unconsciously suppressing, disowning, and denying.

I put my thoughts outside of me by saying them out loud. With this release, the pain would ease. I said, "I don't know why I'm crying; there's no reason for me to be crying! I can't use my mind!" With this sentence releasing from my mouth, I began to question what a mind was. This inquiry led me to discover that the mind was just a concept; there was no such thing as *my* mind.

I felt the need to throw up but wasn't able to. My boss started throwing up, and it felt like she was throwing up for me, what I could not throw up myself. It felt like a massive buildup of energy within me right before she threw up, and then I was relieved once she purged. That was how sensitive I was to energy and how connected we all became, because of taking this plant medicine.

After what felt like an eternity of agony, a slight crack of light made its way into my darkness. It was like I just went on a rollercoaster through hell. I made it through the flips, turns, and twists, and now I was back at the beginning of the ride.

The ride's operator would loosen the straps and locks so I could get off. And then I would step off the ride, kiss the ground, and thank the universe that I made it out alive.

I said to my boss, "That was such a rollercoaster; I'm never doing that again," now that I had regained some control over my mind and emotions again. I laughed wholeheartedly.

I said, "I don't think I will ever be the same again," as I cried tears of gratitude. There was this understanding that something massive had shifted in me. I was never going to be the same person that I was before I left for my trip.

You hear it in many spiritual teachings that children can teach us much about processing emotion. When in need of something, babies will cry—with no concern over whether others are looking at or judging them. As they grow, they are conditioned to hold in or suppress emotions until it's an "okay" time to release them.

Ayahuasca put me in a position to release, to experience *fully*. I had to look at the pain I was suppressing, denying, disowning, and running from for many years. I also had to do all of that in front of a group of people.

It is not a conscious choice that we make—to run from painful emotions. When we touch fire and get burned, we learn to stay away and never do that again. When it comes to spiritual growth, experiencing our pain and dark emotions, can become the doorway to liberation, healing, and freedom.

When we experience a traumatic event, perhaps feeling abandoned by a parent, this can color our emotional lives to begin distrusting others or not allow them to get too close. Not being able to touch the emotion of that inner-child's pain is a state of perpetually living in the "cave of comfort."

At the end of this ceremony, I exclaimed that I would never touch Ayahuasca again. I asked this medicine to teach me how to trust people, and it betrayed me by not giving me a "lovely" experience!

Ayahuasca: Take Two

A week later, I would be sitting in a new Maloca at a retreat center in a different part of the jungle, getting ready to do my second ayahuasca ceremony—never say never, am I right?

Our second ceremony took place at a different retreat center (also with Shipibo shamans). This one, however, was done in the morning.

I came all this way for healing. I wanted to have the courage to dive back into my evolvement—even if it meant facing the "dangerous" waters of agony, once again. My intention for this ceremony was more about my future—I wanted to know my purpose. I wanted to know what I was supposed to teach and contribute to the world. I knew I wanted to be of service, to help others, yet I wasn't exactly sure how I would be doing that in the world.

I will share just a few of the main parts of this ceremony (there are too many parts to cover them all). Once I finally settled into the experience and drank my plant medicine, I laid onto my mat and closed my eyes. I saw visual imagery within my mind's eye (much like a dream).

It began first with seeing myself walking through a forest, surrounded by blue butterflies flying everywhere. I walked along, mesmerized by this sight. Butterflies had much significance to me, as they symbolized transformations and growth.

Very abruptly, in this vision, I was startled by a gun. I was afraid to go into a downward spiral again, like in my first ceremony, so I tried to push this image away. I then felt reassured that this would be okay. I sensed that I should allow it to unfold. I trusted, and the images started to morph.

This gun turned towards me, and I saw myself sitting in front of it, while an unidentifiable person held it from the other side. I accepted my fate; I was ready for death and pulled the gun closer to me. My inner-vision went black, and from this blackness emerged a new scene. I witnessed myself forming inside of a womb. It was a symbol of death and rebirth.

I was in a deep trance, a state of absolute quiet, surrender, and bliss. All noises around me heightened, and my hands, once again, began to move on their own. My hands would point to a particular place within the jungle, and noise would occur in that area. It seemed like a spirit other than myself was moving my body, trying to prove that it was not my consciousness doing so. I could not have known where the next sound was going to come from.

Then this spirit began moving my hands over my body to move or heal any stuck energy (like in my first ceremony). It felt like an energetic surgery was taking place.

When the "surgery" finished, my hands began making movements like they were sewing my body back up to close the energetic opening that was made, to cleanse me.

I was still lying down on my mat with my eyes closed. I saw a book in my mind's eye when I was told clairaudiently that this (book) would be a way I would help others. I heard very loudly and clearly in my head, "You don't need to find the next step; the next step will be revealed to you when you are ready."

Very shortly after, I intuitively knew the ceremony had finished. The shamans stated that we were complete, and I opened my eyes.

The message I received just before the end of the ceremony was telling me to take the next step, not to worry about how I would get to the "bigger picture" of the future. Ayahuasca was telling me to go on the journey. It was not going to show me exactly how it was going to look.

I've learned to take delight in "not knowing." My most enjoyable experiences in life have always been the ones I never planned or expected. Maybe if I knew exactly how everything would pan out, who I would marry, how I would die, and what my life would look like, then I wouldn't ever take steps to get there. It would already be finished.

I wouldn't experience what it was like to move towards it or watch it unfold. Knowing the end would take all the excitement out of it. I never want to know how a movie ends; it's the buildup and the relationship to the characters I develop along the way—that is the point of watching the movie.

If there were no process toward something, there would be no enjoyment of the present moment. The process is the whole reason for existence.

Not only that, but if I was given all the steps I was supposed to take for the rest of my life, I don't think I'd be able to remember past the third step. We must just follow the next step as it intuitively comes.

Family Constellations and Reiki

After one year of working at the crystal shop, the booth rental came to an end. The owner had other ventures she needed to undertake at that point in her life.

Many people might have felt afraid not to have a new job already; I felt like everything would work itself out. I did not know where life was taking me next, but I knew it was going to take me somewhere unplanned, as it had for the past few years. I felt a deep trust that whatever was meant for me to discover next, would reveal itself to me. Whether that came as an idea, an opportunity, or through coming across the right person, I felt reassured that everything would work out.

I began learning online about hypnotherapy, and was looking into beginning schooling to become a certified hypnotherapist. Months after the store closed, I thought of my previous boss and asked her if she was open to taking people for Kambo ceremonies; she was.

After my ceremony, she told me about her friend, named Sonya Arias. They were going to be facilitating a ceremony together, that weekend. I felt I should be there. That was when I met the woman who would become a close friend, roommate, teacher, and mentor to me.

Currently (as I am writing this book), I'm training with her as both a Family Constellations Facilitator and a Reiki practitioner.

Family Constellations is a methodology that helps to reveal or change unhealthy familial patterns. Those patterns that were passed down to us can often influence and determine how our lives progress.

This practice works on the basis that through the DNA we received from our parents (and the family members before them), we inherit life patterns and subconscious beliefs.

Through experiencing this work, I have witnessed and become aware of how actions, traumas, and suppressed emotions of those who came before us, primarily affect the choices we make in our lives. The objective of the work is to witness these patterns. It dives into psychotherapy, trauma, addictions, grief, coping and defense mechanisms, relationships, family systems, and esoteric views on inherited trauma passed on from ancestors and family members (the family system).

Once becoming aware of the unhealthy patterns, that acknowledgment opens the door to freedom for the client to live their lives freely and differently. There is a saying in Family Constellations that goes, "It ends with me."

This means that, "Because I have become aware of, acknowledged, accepted, and forgiven the patterns that were passed to me, I am now able to end the pattern. I can create a new path in the world, that honors my own highest good and the highest good of others."

The founder of Family Constellations was named Bert Hellinger. He brought together many modalities, which he learned within his lifetime. His work stems from years of learning and observing the Zulu tribe in Africa, his time learning about families in the Anglican clergy, his studies in NLP (neurolinguistic programming), psychology, and hypnotherapy (among other learnings). His work is also derived from teachers like Milton Erickson and Virginia Satir.

Explaining his work could become a whole other book. Bert Hellinger has various books teaching these concepts. However, I'd like to point out that experiential learning goes above concepts and the thinking mind. Experiencing the presence felt in an actual constellation and seeing what the field can reveal to you (or about you) is a mind-boggling, otherworldly experience.

I'll briefly describe what goes on during a workshop (as I have learned it from my teacher). Every constellation is different and particular to the specific client. As a general example, this is what could transpire:

> The facilitator and client each sit in front of a group of people. Everyone sits in chairs aligned to form a circle. The client comes in with an issue and states it in front of the group. The facilitator goes into a state of deep presence. They tap into an energy field (sometimes called the morphogenic field) with trust and surrender. They allow the field to move them to take specific actions.

They may be moved to bring up people from the circle to represent people within the family system. If the client comes in and says, "I'm having issues in my relationship and want to work on whatever keeps me from having a healthy relationship," the facilitator may ask someone to represent the client, someone to represent her boyfriend, and a person to represent each of her parents. Then the field would move through each of the participants. They may experience the emotions, thoughts, or experiences of those whom they are representing—even though they know nothing about the people or the relationships between them.

Stuck energy in the form of suppressed emotions, like anger, tears of sadness, or grief, may also move through the participants. The field is bringing these stuck energies to the surface, to be acknowledged, accepted, and moved. The practitioner can also be inspired to say certain sentences to help the energy to process or move.

In this example, the field could reveal that the client unknowingly took on the energies of her parents—the suppressed traumas or resentments, and chose a partner aligned with the energy that she was attracting. Through the work in the constellation, the client can become aware of this and choose differently. Since the energy was moved in the constellation, the interaction in the relationship often shifts, or she attracts a new mate that is more in alignment with her.

This is a very general explanation of an experience, but I wanted to give you a picture of what can be experienced. It is fascinating to see people accurately depict what goes on within a family without knowing anything about them.

Doing my own work, seeing my coping mechanisms at play, and becoming aware of when I am disassociating (running from pain) has opened my eyes to just how unconscious we can be of our coping methods. We are blind to it until someone comes along to show us when we are doing it.

Family Constellations has connected me back to accepting who I come from, and forgiving the patterns that were passed down through generations. It has also taught me about compassion and love, for people who have done the most harm in the world. I've learned the power of the subconscious mind, how what we have not or cannot look at, is why we make the decisions we do. It has given me the freedom to take my power back. It put me in the driver's seat to alter my own reality and perceptions, which can lead me into a new life.

The other healing modality which I learned from her (Reiki) is a form of energetic work. The kind I learned about (Usui Reiki) originated in Japan by a man named Mikao Usui.

Reiki uses the energetic frequency of unconditional love. It is run through the recipient's body to bring their energetic and physical body back into its natural state of harmony and balance. When the body is in harmony, the natural tendency is for it to heal itself, and many physical ailments are thought to come from energetic imbalances.

Through these trainings, and living with her to learn from her, I received so many invaluable life lessons about myself, helping others, ethics, and business.

Life will take you along a wild ride; sometimes, it seems like without your consent. At the start of my journey, when I took that first step to walk into libraries to read about dead people, I couldn't have predicted that it would develop into me going on a trip to do Ayahuasca or to see sights like Machu Picchu (a photo that was once just a dream on my vision board).

I never planned to initiate a "spiritual path." I never intended to meet someone in college who would begin the unfolding of many beautiful experiences, adventures, and friends. I never planned to meet these people; meeting them was just the next step of my unfolding journey.

As Ayahuasca said to me, "You don't need to find the next step; it will be revealed to you when you are ready."

So far, it was just one small step that led to many more steps, sometimes even leaps.

This journey (and my experiences) has led me to some beliefs or principles about living life fully and happily. I will share with you just a few of what I call "Life's Secrets" that I've come across along the way.

CHAPTER 3

Everything Happens *for* You

I decided to go to a botanical garden in the summer of 2021, so I could be out in nature. I found one in San Diego. As I walked along the trails of this garden, I passed by ponds filled with Koi fish. I stepped along pebbled pathways, surrounded by trees filled with Sakura flowers in bloom, and found myself drawn towards one specific tree.

Upon approaching it, I noticed a plaque on the floor beneath it. It described the tree's origins. "Peace Tree" was written out in big gold letters. Under that name, it explained that this tree, along with 15 others, was given to this garden. All of them were trees that survived the atomic bombing of Hiroshima in Japan.

An organization set up this distribution of trees to give a message of hope, life, and peace, to the world. As I stood before this tree, I contemplated the true message of it.

I found it to be a physical representation of the love, unity, and humanity that is possible even between "enemies." This tree also gave the message that life continues to grow and evolve, even after much destruction. This tree was enormous, mature, and intricate, even though it originated around disastrous circumstances.

I have a story I'm reminded of whenever I think of this tree.

A man was in a tumultuous marriage that ended. In this marriage, he focused his full attention on being a good partner and father, yet it seemed that everything he did was never enough in the critical eyes of his wife.

He made decisions that brought him into a situation where he allowed others to consume his whole sense of worthiness. Because of the circumstances within that relationship, he became incredibly insecure and unsure of his passion or purpose in life.

He internalized their disapproval as something being wrong with *him*. He became what everyone else wanted him to be and couldn't fathom who *he* wanted to be.

Because of growing up in a family that frowned upon divorce, deciding to part ways with his then-wife would be seen by everyone around him as shameful. Life put him into a circumstance that caused massive discomfort; he would be going against everything he had learned since he was a child.

Within the next few weeks, this already shaky marriage ended because of circumstances out of his control.

He felt as if he were a free man, with all possibilities for his future now open for something brand new. From then on, he had the freedom to be, or become, whomever he wanted to become.

That was the moment that his journey towards self-worth and living for himself began. It was *his* moment of "break-down" to "break-through." Many years later, he was happy, doing what he loved, and was now grateful for that hardship.

With some time having passed and hindsight, anybody who has grown or evolved from a massively "contrasting" experience will tell you that they are immensely grateful for the moment that they, at one point in time, cursed.

Even a tree that came from a bombing, surrounded by destruction, continues to live on; it has the capacity for new expansion and a new environment.

The Tree of "Struggle"

During a trip to Alaska (my Abraham-Hicks cruise), when we stopped in a city called Skagway, I got onto a train for an excursion. It was called the White Pass Railroad. People built this railroad during the Klondike Gold Rush.

At that time, there was talk of riches and gold to be mined in that area. This trail was one of the ways to get in—and it was a perilous route: men risked their lives in search of these riches.

As our train gradually increased in elevation, I sat, peering through the window, admiring the Alaskan mountains, streams, and lush greenery. Over the train's speaker, a woman shared facts with us about the history of this railroad. "Take a look at those trees out there."

She explained that these Alaskan trees had intricate root systems that adapted to the changing conditions of the external world. When storms would come, the trees responded by growing deeper roots into the ground to withstand the next storm.

Evolution and adaptation are the tree's response to great chaos. A new form begins. That form is one that could not have existed without the storm. *All* life forms evolve into a new and improved form when placed under immense pressure.

Pain, sickness, and loss—these are inevitable within this reality. Without pressure, there is no need to grow. If all were perfect in one's life, complacency and stagnation would be the result, not evolvement. If nothing ever needed to change, why would you change it?

Like that old saying, "If it ain't broke, don't fix it." Thank goodness things break because it leaves the door open for improvement—and the creation of life itself.

Wabi-Sabi

At a day-long silent meditation retreat at the Los Angeles Peace and Awareness Labyrinth and Gardens, I learned about Wabi-Sabi. We experienced many forms of meditation, one of which included a Japanese tea ceremony. The facilitator shared with us the intricacy, sacredness, and meaning of this ceremony.

Wabi-Sabi is a Japanese aesthetic and philosophy, which teaches to look at life through the eyes of appreciation for imperfection, impermanence, transience, and weathering.

During a tea ceremony, the teacups and utensils used are supposed to attain weathering, and look imperfect with all their character (through dents, cracks, or scratches). It is the view that imperfections are what gives something its beauty. They asked us to reflect on the teacups' flaws with reverence.

A tree that shows more weathering tells the story of each storm it has endured. This speaks of the resilience it must have had to withstand such a tumultuous environment. It brings uniqueness into that one specific tree. It tells of the diversity that sets it apart from all others.

There is a beauty to the wrinkle lines on one's face, a beauty to the smile lines—these are the evidence of a life filled with many laughs. A flower must grow from a seed into a seedling; its stem must reach out of the soil until it blooms fully. Then it must die so that new flowers may come into the world. This evolution is what makes eternity possible. I've never seen a flower hang on for dear life because it wants to stay in full bloom for eternity.

There is no secret "youth juice" that we can take for eternal youth. There are no surgeries that can completely reverse the natural process of growing, withering, and inevitably dying.

Perhaps we could get enough surgery to make us look younger for ten years, but this is a very temporary "fix" for a "problem" that we cannot halt. No amount of money would allow any of us to become indestructible.

Destruction of life comes with the bringing of life. The two are synonymous with each other. Old forms are lost so that new ones can develop—perhaps that is why each subsequent generation seems to change the world in a new way.

After the death of a particular chapter in our lives, new growth can begin. It does not minimize the pain of loss, but it magnetizes the fact that much beauty can come out of destruction.

If this evolution didn't happen, maybe we would all still be cavemen somewhere. We can't know what *would* have happened, but I would bet that it would've led to much less evolvement than where we currently stand.

Love comes for a moment; then it is lost. Life comes for a moment, then death must follow. Time is there for one moment—then the moment must pass. In these instances of destruction, is a moment where rebuilding can commence. A tree will cut off its nutrient supply to the fruit whose time has passed. This inevitable dying and release, makes room for the tree to continue its renewal process each year.

There's a beauty in garnering deeper roots of resilience to extend help to another (whose place we were once in). Moments of hardship can lead to gaining much wisdom or compassion for others in the place we were once in. Our pain can be our greatest teacher. It pushes us to the most significant possibilities for growth.

The Mesmerizing Rose

The crystal shop I worked at was a small booth in an outdoor mall. Right next to the booth, big red roses would grow each spring. During the spring I spent working there, one rose outgrew them all.

This rose was prepared to grow massively tall from the moment that it sprouted. It was about as tall as me, or even a bit taller (I'm a little over five feet).

Many people that walked past our booth would stop to have a look at this gigantic rose. Parents would pick their children up to smell it and marvel at its uniqueness. Men and women would tilt it towards themselves, look at me, and say things like, "I've never seen a rose like that, how beautiful!"

I was so grateful to be working at that booth during that time. I got to be a part of this rose's life cycle and watch as people gawked over its loveliness.

This rose taught me much about life. It prepared for a lovely existence by first making sure its stem was thick enough to reach as close to the heavens as possible. It evolved gradually in its right timing until its full bloom.

Then it lived in its fullest manifestation, allowed others to be captivated by its beauty, and moved on when the timing was right, to let other roses have their time. I was able to be a witness to its beginning, its growing process, its bloom, the people it encountered, and eventually, its end.

The memory it has given to me and those who got to encounter it—lives on eternally. Now it will live on forever in this book and in *your* mind.

Kintsugi

Kintsugi is another Japanese idea, similar to Wabi-Sabi. It highlights the possibility for renewal that comes from brokenness. It's believed that this originated from Shogun Ashikaga Yoshimasa[1] in the 1400s when he shattered a tea bowl.

When the bowl was repaired using metal staples and sent back to him, he ordered the fixers to find a more aesthetically pleasing way to fix the brokenness. Their fix was to pour gold between the cracks. The shiny metal kept it together in a way that was pleasurable to look at.

Thus was the birth of the art of "Kintsugi," where something is purposely (or accidentally) shattered. From that moment of *apparent* destruction, a new form becomes possible (the reason for its newfound beauty). All is not lost when something has shattered.

The cracks from the break are still there; they are a vital element of the "new beauty" as much as the gold is. If the shattering never happened, there would be no cracks to fill. You could not add the gold *unless* the brokenness came first.

A broken form isn't a reason to "throw something away"—it is the reason for its transformation, improvement, and growth. To further dive into this idea of Wabi-Sabi and Kintsugi, I want to share an experience I had in an improv class.

I decided to take a class like this—not because I wanted to be an actor, but because I wanted to experience being on stage and to become more comfortable with public speaking.

Improvisational acting is a form of performing that is entirely on the spot. While on stage, scene partners take suggestions from the audience. These suggestions could include the location of where the actors are (like at a carnival). They would then play out a scene on the stage from this suggestion. Many times, it turns into comedy.

The performers form the characters at that moment—no pre-planning, no time to think, no lines, it just arises and evolves. If the audience gives the scene partners the location of the "carnival," one of them may take on a child's character, and the other a clown or a parent. You get the picture.

During one of our classes, our teacher explained, "This class is about failing. Sometimes the scene will not work, sometimes you will say something wrong, sometimes you will feel like you said something dumb or like people were judging you for it. In this work, that is inevitable."

He then said, "If it doesn't work, there is another scene coming. When we fail, we don't go home thinking, 'I could've done that better, or I shouldn't have said that.' You can't change that moment, even if you wanted to."

When our teacher said this, it occurred to me that failing in life is like that. I have "failed" in this *current* present moment. A business venture didn't work out. I lost an investment. A relationship didn't work out; I said the wrong thing to someone I loved or hurt someone's feelings.

It is one scene out of many subsequent scenes which are to come. It cannot be changed even if you wanted to change it. I know that if I have seemingly messed up in life, I can choose to make it better than the last scene. I can use that failure to create a better scene in the next "character" that I play.

Improvisational acting also forces you to stay present within each moment. You have no idea what your partner will say next; you have no idea where the scene will go when you begin. Surrender to the moment is required, no matter how it is unfolding. If the scene is going badly—the show must go on, because time does not stand still.

This same presence is required in our day-to-day lives, whether we're in the best place of our lives, or the worst place. Presence allows us to let go of the previous moment and ride the waves of life as they present themselves. We must always move forward into the new.

When my life, seemingly, shattered as a teenager—this was the moment that I poured gold into the cracks. When I experienced sickness, loss, grief, and pain, I could not comprehend the gems that could be born from those moments. I was oblivious to the strength that would arise and the new self that would happen *because* of it.

Had I died on the day I decided I should no longer be on this earth, I wouldn't have had the opportunity to come to understand what life *could* become. Had I not let that scene be what it was and decided on creating a new one out of the next segment of my life, well, you would not be reading this book.

Impermanence

When I was attending Michael's psychic and trance classes, I would leave home early to first visit the beach, as it was close to the class's location. I would take a book with me, sit on the pier overlooking the water, read, and watch the sun as it was setting.

One time, as I walked along the pier, I looked down towards the shoreline. I noticed a vast, intricate masterpiece taking form.

A group of people diligently worked to create a mandala made of colorful sand—and they were doing so, right up against waves that would inevitably wash away their creation. I thought to myself, "Why would someone create a beautiful work of art, just so that waves could destroy it?"

I contemplated the reason why anybody would do this. Then I thought, "Is this not true of every physical creation, every flower, every animal, every human, every building, *everything*?"

Are we not masterful creations, creating masterful works of art (which are our lives), only to all come to an inevitable end once we leave this world? Are we not creating and decorating homes that we will not keep forever? Are we not making and planting gardens that we cannot take with us when moving to a new home?

There is a story of a man who amassed great wealth within his lifetime—billions of dollars. He was a philanthropist throughout his life, donating significant amounts to charities. As his death approached (in his old age), his goal was to be alive to (happily) watch as **all** the wealth he amassed in his lifetime was given to charities.

There are many people who, upon facing their demise, realize that they cannot take what they have with them when they depart this world. They recognize the futile pointlessness of happiness coming from anything of this world. What is its actual value if you cannot keep it?

The material world is ever-changing. Many religions of the world speak of non-attachment to the material world. It is in the teachings of Jesus to "Be in the world, but not of the world."

The Buddha, who came from a wealthy upbringing, gave up his worldly possessions, went on a journey to understand the meaning of life, and became enlightened.

I am not suggesting that it is everyone's purpose in life to become a monk or sell everything they own and go traveling in a van—in fact doing these things is not a sure-fire way to reach enlightenment.

True equanimity in one's life does not imply cynicism or carelessness. It's not a nihilistic worldview that knows "all things are damned, so none of it matters." It is an acceptance of the inevitable, and this opens the door to *true* living.

It is the understanding that nothing is permanent and that all experiences come with good and bad—and therefore, this life is precious.

Viewing the world through impermanence does not mean it's unwise to find joy in the "highs" of life because they will end. It doesn't mean we shouldn't seek to create beautiful things, manifestations, or material objects in the world. Instead, it is a state of freedom in the present moment, which allows us to experience those highs for as long as they last, with the understanding that it will come to an end one day.

It is like thoroughly enjoying your child's first steps and reveling in that present moment. All while knowing that you will never get to see that moment ever again, but more moments of pride and joy will continue as your child grows up and goes on their own life's journey, with you as their guide.

The bittersweet is what makes life full. The complete enjoyment of a single meal, while you are eating it, is much more satisfying, than spending your meal thinking about what you will be eating during your next meal. Savoring day-to-day moments—like your child's first steps—is a fulfilled life.

Life will always wash away the present moment to create new expansion and evolvement. Moments can be enjoyed as if they were mandalas created right up against the ocean, next to waves that are sure to wash them away.

The Sun Comes Back

I love to sit at the beach and watch the sunset. My favorite part is when the sun touches the horizon as it slowly fades behind the mountains or the ocean.

During one of my trips to the beach, I was sitting, watching the sun fade away. I thought about how lovely it was that the sky was constantly in flux. Each day the sun went up and back down so that I could see a new sunset.

Imagine it's the first time you've ever seen a sunset, and you don't know if the sun will ever rise again. You are enthralled, captivated even, to see this breathtaking sight, with its glorious purples, pinks, and oranges. It's like a magnificent painting that your lucky eyes are blessed to witness.

Then, suddenly it vanishes, there's no light left, and the darkness begins to fall over the earth. You feel agony for having lost the sun, this beautiful scene that one moment ago blessed you with its beauty.

So, you cry in agony, become depressed because it was so beautiful, and it's so painful to have lost it. You genuinely believe you will never get to see it again (because this is your first time experiencing darkness).

You spend the whole night in deep pain for losing this beautiful sight. Hours later, a sudden ray of light fills the darkness. Until the light completely consumes it. Now you can enjoy the light once more!

Then inevitably, it falls again, and darkness returns. You can either find solace in being within the night momentarily, knowing that it will pass and that it is a necessary part of creating a sunset or sunrise. The darkness works synonymously with the light to shift the sky each day.

Or you can suffer during every moment of darkness during every night until the sun shines once again.

The only way to delight in a sunset is if the sun goes away for the night. The only way that a person can know happiness is if they have known sadness. The only way that they can appreciate life is if they know there is death.

Knowing these come hand in hand can bring solace in our darker moments. It can bring hope for a better tomorrow. To suffer within it or not, is a choice that we each must make in our lives.

Darkness and storms can cause you to grow deeper roots into the ground. In this awareness, it is possible to reach out of the earth to create an even stronger and thicker stem, to bloom into a giant rose that others can enjoy the beauty of, and then to move into a new form when your time has finished.

Chapter 4

The Eternal Process of Evolvement

At about twenty-three years old, I went to a live concert featuring one of my favorite artists. As he was on the stage, he began talking to the crowd about how he was living on his friend's couch at one point in his life.

He explained that at that time of his life, he had no money to buy food. Because of this, he had to "humble himself" to ask a friend to buy him a jar of peanut butter.

He was only just beginning his work as an artist. He had faith and belief in his dreams, but he had no evidence in front of him to prove that they would become real.

He *dreamed* of being a touring artist and of people loving his work so much that they became dedicated listeners. This man was so sure that this imaginary tomorrow would be the end to his suffering.

Certainly (to him), his suffering came from the fact that he needed money but did not have any and that he wanted people to enjoy his art, but very few people were listening. He thought that he would become happy once he finally had those things.

Now that he was standing in that dream years later (touring and playing his music for people who loved it), he said he would never have imagined that it would come with its own hardships as well. He was right there standing in front of a cheering crowd, telling us that this dream he once desired so badly, was not all that he had hoped it would be.

He spoke of industry experts who wanted to manipulate and alter his art to sell better to masses of people. He explained that he had to fight to remain authentic to his self-expression, or he would have had to lose *himself,* pleasing others for monetary benefit.

He also talked of the strife that touring caused in his romantic relationships. It became hard to maintain close relationships because of him always being "on the move." He described the beautiful aspects that the materialization of his dreams brought to his life as well (it was not solely negative, as he was doing what he loved).

THE ETERNAL PROCESS OF EVOLVEMENT

Upon experiencing the reality that he at one point only dreamed of, he realized that there was no destination to get to, where he would feel, "I have arrived." No tomorrow was going to be a better one than today.

It reminds me of the idea of parched men in the desert. Ones who would walk thirstily, *direly* seeking water, hoping for a better "later." They would begin seeing a body of water off in the distance, unaware that this was a mirage. The promise of a better later, where water would be in their mouths, would cause them to crawl toward this apparent body of water.

They would have no clue that they were *walking* toward an illusory body of water, a mirage. They were chasing something they were *sure* they could see with their eyes!

They would spend their lives in pursuit of it, never having gotten to it, because it was never "over there." It was simply a mind-made idea of a futuristic "better" present moment.

For many people, it is an everyday occurrence to "put off" happiness until tomorrow. It is as if many believe that one day, they will finally arrive at some imaginary destination where everything will *finally* be all well and finished. Finally, maybe one day, the perfect reality will quench their "thirst," and they won't want for anything more.

Those who experience the full manifestation of what they dreamed of having, are lucky to realize that happiness is independent from their outer circumstances. They can then come to understand the true meaning of *being* in their life's existence. Many people die having never come to this realization. They die seeking water they will never reach.

The Fleeting Present Moment

While I was still in college (maybe around 20 years old), I sat in my backyard reading. I looked up at a hummingbird feeder hanging from the patio in front of me.

I quietly watched a little hummingbird drink nectar. Once finished, it came up to me at eye level to check me out for a few seconds. I sat there admiring it, delighting in this moment.

I remained as quiet and still as possible so I wouldn't scare it away sooner. If I moved or tried to reach out to hold onto it, the moment would have ceased to be.

You cannot grasp or contain a hummingbird— so a hummingbird briefly choosing to delight in a small moment with you is a moment to be cherished.

We can hold onto nothing in life—all of it is fleeting. We've learned to grasp onto, to reach out for happiness tomorrow, like the men in the desert. All while it is always sitting there fluttering its wings, in the present moment.

The Expansive Nature of Reality

A man once told me about how he would go to a dealership frequently to look at his dream car. He wanted to manifest this specific one; he thought, "I will be the world's happiest man forever if I could just get that car." He would marvel at it and imagine that one day it would be his.

He "made a deal with God" in his head: "God, if you give me this car, I will never ask you for anything ever again. I will be happy for eternity."

After some time passed, his father knew how much his son dreamed of having this car and decided to buy it for him.

The son was ecstatic. Yes! This is what he always wanted; God answered his prayers. Now that it was his, he opened the door and drove his first drive home in his dream car.

He parked it in his garage. The moment he got out and shut the car door, he recalled saying in his head, "God, I'm so sorry, I lied to you; this is not going to be the last thing I ask of you."

This moment was the moment he understood the joy of moving towards creating something. Even after his dream came true, he *still* wanted to make more in this world.

What if, when you were a baby, your cells said, "You know what, I like being like this. I think I'll stop here, and I'll stay a baby forever."

Imagine you never held the desire to stand up to walk, or to keep trying even though you kept falling. With enough belief in your ability to walk, you knew that you could do it. You knew that even though you were falling and wobbly now, you would eventually get there.

The unknown, and the possibility for new experiences, *is* the reason for existence. Let's take a shirt in a store, for example. You want it so badly, it fits so nicely, and you love the way it looks and feels between your fingertips. You say to yourself, "I must have it," and so you talk yourself into buying it. You wear it any chance you get because you love how confident you feel, and people compliment you.

Years later, you see this shirt in the back of your closet and think to yourself, "Wow, I remember how badly I wanted this thing, and now it's just sitting here. I've forgotten about it. I never wear it; how about I give it away because I no longer need it."

Sure, having something new that you wanted causes you to be happy for a moment. But a shirt is just a shirt. There are so many other desires you have; there are so many more clothes to wear. There is an expanding you—whose taste extends to places it's not been yet. A painter creates paintings for the creating part and will not stop after just one painting.

That is because he enjoys the process of making it how he wants it, for the fun of creating. He doesn't do it to say, "This is it; this is the only one I'll paint for the rest of my life because it's just right."

Once a flower has undergone its process toward blooming, there is no regression possible. It cannot reverse itself back into a seedling—this is the natural process of evolution and growth.

There is no standing still. There is no looking back. The rose does not look at its old leaves and say, "Wait just a minute, I think I'll redo that." It keeps growing for the joy of creation. There is no pause, rewind, or fast forward—there is simply *now*.

The desires possible for one's life are endless, and they will continue to expand because nothing will stay still, and nothing will ever be "perfectly" perfect. Perfect would imply completeness, which would lead to an "end."

Embracing the Unknown

Alan Watts has a story[1] in which he talks about "the unknown" by comparing it to a dream world. In it, he asks his audience to imagine that they could dream each night, whatever they wanted to. He explains that these dreamers could fit 75 years into just that one night.

At the beginning of this experience of "desire fulfilling dreams," they would first satisfy every wish or desire they could think of. They could "manifest" their cars, dream homes, vacations, relationships—anything that they even slightly desired to experience.

After many nights of having had everything they could ever want, they would become increasingly bored—because they would know exactly what comes next. Their dreams would be under their complete control.

Because of their boredom, they would decide to instead, have a dream that they could not control anymore.

They would begin desiring the circumstance of having dreams where they wouldn't know the dream's outcome anymore. It would feel like an electrifying gamble that tossed all possibilities up into the air.

After this taste of having complete control of their dreams' outcomes, this new and exciting unknown factor would become a "breath of fresh air." Imagine that, being so used to having all control, then experiencing the contrast of the exciting "unexpected." How delighted you would be to finally not know what was coming!

These dream-dwellers would keep deciding to have dreams that they didn't have control over—and they'd find themselves back right where they started before they began wanting the power of controlling their dreams. They would be living in the very same world they started with, blessing the life that they once wanted so badly to change.

The Eternal Process of Evolvement

Many of us *think* we would like to have all of our wishes fulfilled. We think it would make life much more enjoyable if all our desires were right at our fingertips. It is like looking out at a better tomorrow, all while missing out on where we are currently standing. Always trying to grab hold of an imaginary better moment, while living in this perpetual state of "not enough yet," can create a life of constant dissatisfaction.

- "I will be happy when I get the raise."
- "I will be happy when my lover comes to me, and I get married."
- "I will be happy when I'm famous, and people give me recognition for my work."
- "I will be happy when I have enough money in my bank account to do anything I want with my money."

Sometimes this searching is very subtle—and we don't realize we are searching until we finally have those things we thought we wanted. We realize, "This is not everything I thought it would be." Present moment discontent, such as this, further magnifies the story of the men in the desert, or the man up on the stage realizing it wasn't everything he wanted it to be, or the man who thought a mustang would complete his life.

A desire for a reality other than the one we are in, can become exaggerated, particularly when things are going "wrong."

When times are uncertain in one's life, where the outcomes are unknown (and *seem* likely only to turn out negative), there is a great possibility for the mind to become catapulted into anxiety or dread about where the future will lead. The fight or flight response can kick into high gear because of a perceived threat. It is much like a human being chased by a tiger, but in modern times, the tiger is our boss, or the next payment we have to make by the end of the month.

Whether or not it is a life or death situation, the person's perception of the circumstance can cause their body to respond as if there is truly a threat.

In times of uncertainty, which seem negative, the unknown future can do one of two things:

- It can take you down—hurl you into fear, dread, anxiety, impulsive reactivity, and massive amounts of insanity/pain. This mind state can then lead to action taken out of suffering (which would lead to even more pain/suffering to oneself and all others around).
- Or, it can cause you to become immensely present so that you can take whatever effective action is needed—without the mental projections of the worst-case scenario happening.

Many spiritual teachings talk about "non-attachment." I would suggest that this does not mean "have no desires" or "don't enjoy physical objects." Instead, contemplating these objects' importance can allow us to uncover a deeper layer of our "spiritual nature."

The Eternal Process of Evolvement

Imagine a man driving on a highway, headed towards large mountains in the distance, many miles away. Now, imagine that, suddenly, a huge rainstorm comes thundering over him. He smacks his steering wheel while saying through clenched teeth, "This rainstorm is the worst thing that could have ever happened to me!"

Imagine he stops driving. He pulls over, gets out of the car, and walks into the rain. Now he's standing there getting drenched by this storm, yelling up to the heavens, "Why must you do this to me? I did nothing to deserve this!" The fact that he is now wet is even more irritating to him, because now he has to get back into his car and ruin his seats. He took action out of his frustration, which led to more frustration.

He could very well choose to keep yelling for hours at this uncontrollable factor, and the situation would certainly not change until nature "finished." He cannot tell the weather what to do, and he cannot throw his clothes into the dryer at that moment. He has the choice to surrender, or he has the option to keep on with his frustration. He can live his entire life that way until the moment of his demise.

On this same highway, at the same time, another man in a different car also notices the rain. He chooses to pull over, sits on the side of the road in his warm (and dry) car, and reads a book. He sits there peacefully, waiting for the storm to pass. Once it does, he continues with his drive.

These were the same life circumstances; however, they were two separate reactions and two distinct experiences of this reality. To one, it means that someone is punishing him. The other understands that it will be just a moment before the storm passes; it's not personal. One reaction is not the "right" or "wrong" way to experience the situation—there is free will for anyone to experience his reality however he chooses.

The mind can quickly become a prison, and a person can continue with this suffering (as many do) for the duration of their whole life existence. That is unless he chooses to become the driver of his mental state, regardless of the external situation, not the one being driven.

From this place, effective action for true change is more likely to come about—because it is a solution-oriented action, not an impulsive action taken out of frustration.

The Boy Who Lost His Horse

Many people I have met along this path of unfoldment, have talked to me about an ancient Chinese parable.

A young man loses his horse. As a response to this incident, everyone around consoles him except for his father. He instead suggests that maybe it was a good thing it happened to his son.

After some time passes, the initially "lost" horse comes back with a group of many other horses.

Onlookers tell the young man how great it was that this happened to him. What a lucky young boy for having lost one horse and then gaining a whole herd of them! His father suggests that maybe this would instead bring bad luck. The boy goes riding on one of these new horses, falls, and breaks a leg.

Again, the onlookers console him—how unlucky, he hurt his leg! Once again, the father tells him that maybe it's a good thing it happened. A war breaks out, and the able men must go to war. The son and father don't have to go into this war because of the son's broken leg. Yet again, these men are seen as "lucky."

Just as the good things that happen to us bring bad things, the bad things that happen to us can bring good things.

Did you get into a relationship? How fantastic for you, since you have wanted one for so long! Now that you have someone to love, you are so "lucky"! You two got into a fight, are unhappy, or you're getting divorced? How "unlucky" is that? I'm so sorry! Oh, but now you've met someone even better who you love more now? That's amazing!

Having lots of money seems to be a good thing. That would stop the suffering of one who has no money. Now that he has money, he can have anything he wants! Oh, but now that he's wealthy, people are going after him to get some of it? That's horrible.

Life comes with these ups and downs, innately. Life comes with the full spectrum of contrasting experiences.

Good can lead to bad, and bad can lead to good. Just as stated earlier in the book—the hardships in one's life typically become the reason they become a new version of themselves, which developed because of the storm.

Chapter 5

Strength in Surrender

Here's one of those cliché spiritual quotes for you that I am sure many of you have already heard: "The tree that bends doesn't break."

When I hear this quote (or variations of it), I think of a monk up in the Himalayas, speaking to someone who has traveled to him from another country. The traveler stands before the monk looking for the secrets to "enlightenment." Then he gives this monk a list of everything going wrong in his life—so he gets how much he *needs* the secret to end his troubles.

The monk stands there silently, intently listening, with a smile on his face. Then finally, the man stops rambling this long laundry list of everything going wrong to listen to what the monk has to say. "Tell me how to fix it," he pleads. In response to this man's plea, the monk looks him in the eyes as he says calmly, simply, and wisely, "The tree that bends doesn't break."

The man looks at him, perplexed and annoyed. Then he says defiantly, "So you're telling me I came here for mystical advice, spent thousands of dollars to get to you, hiked this giant mountain, and all you have to tell me is *'the tree that bends doesn't break'?*"

These are simple words. It seems like advice that will not help when you are in the throes of outer chaos. But yes, the tree that bends will withstand much more outer chaos than the hard and brittle tree, which resists the chaos. The wind will take down the one who is unwilling to flow with it.

Every single one of us will face challenges. There is no way around it; there is only the choice to fight with the waves coming at you, or to allow them to take you somewhere new. No matter the outer circumstance, there is always a choice to focus internally on present moment awareness. The internal realm need not be tainted or affected by outer circumstances unless one's sense of self derives from the external world.

The eternal self is untouchable, no matter the circumstance. This self is *not* your belongings, monetary wealth, status, notoriety, or anything of the physical world. With this realization comes true freedom.

From Prison to Liberation

While in college, I took a creative writing class. That teacher (and the school) set up a seminar for the poet, Jimmy Santiago Baca, to come and speak to us. I didn't know what it would be about, nor had I ever heard of him. I felt called to be at this seminar.

As he stood in front of the class, he introduced himself and showed us videos and pictures depicting his childhood. This man experienced an extremely tumultuous upbringing that included abuse, parental abandonment, homelessness, drug dealing, being shot, and incarceration. I am sure there were many other experiences in his life that I am not aware of.

He was exposed to a cruel and unkind world from the moment that he was born. When you hear stories such as this one, you can see just how much our environment can define who we eventually become.

Consequently, Baca was incarcerated during his early twenties, after which he was sent to a maximum-security prison. While there, he experienced much mistreatment. He was abused and repeatedly put into isolation rooms, where he had to sit in a black room for long periods.

During this seminar, Baca explained what it was like to live in perpetual darkness, inside an enclosed space, without human contact. He had to step outside of himself so that he didn't lose his mind. It was just him and his mind—nowhere to run, no way to hide from himself, no T.V. to pass the time, no music to distract him.

When a human being gets stripped of all capacity to change his outer circumstances, his inner world becomes the only world he has any control of. Insanity or mind-liberation become the only possible avenues to choose from.

This man lived in an actual, physical prison, which he had no choice but to "submit" to. A massive state of surrender was vital to his sanity and was the only clear opening towards sovereignty.

Sometimes we grow up in circumstances that lead us to become "monsters." Perhaps it is because a child grows up around poverty, crime, and pain that they will learn to do such things as well. It is not to excuse this behavior, but simply to bring light to the fact that everything begins somewhere. It is to understand the human behind the act, the reason someone became a "monster."

Surrendering to life's uncontrollable circumstances, and beginning personal inner-work, can lead to massive transformation. If the inner changes, then the outer must as well. Different actions create different outcomes—and, therefore, a new life. A "new" inner world born out of choice to change oneself would lead to a new way of being in the world.

Now, back to this story of Baca. While in prison, he began learning to read, something he never had the privilege of doing in his formative years. He started this self-teaching by fervently studying a dictionary. That then led him to read poetry and actual books. Eventually, he ventured into writing his *own* pieces.

This newfound learning and passion for communication sparked his love for writing in a way that could transform another human being. He saw that words could inspire people to emotion and new ways of being in the world. His words could make a difference in the life of another human being.

I once heard one of his stories, which touched my heart deeply. He said that one of his fellow inmates (a man raised to become racist toward Latinos) asked him to help write a poem or letter for his mother. When the man received this work, he was incredibly moved. He felt an appreciation for Baca's art and how he could put words together to create an emotion. This small gesture connected two men who would otherwise be enemies in the outside world.

They could have very well come to hate each other; had they not been in prison, they could have done much harm to one another. The world taught them to misunderstand each other, use violence instead of words, and scream with anger instead of communicating with love.

This moment helped Baca to understand the power of influence that words had. He saw how he could change lives through words, how people could connect when they communicated. He also saw how violence was a largely unproductive method of "changing something" compared to this way of communicating.

Learning this power was what would give him the key to a new life. In this experience, he not only discovered the power of words, but he also unearthed his awareness of his ability to direct his mind, no matter the circumstance. He became a free man because of being in prison. Odd, isn't it?

His upbringing, which contained much violence, also taught him how unawareness was primarily the cause of much suffering within the world. He was only a product of his environment. He was acting out of the awareness he was taught through that upbringing.

Since his release from prison, he went on to write many awarded pieces. Baca also became a professor at Yale for some time. In one interview, he explained that once he began teaching there, he observed that many of his students were in a much larger mental prison than he was ever in. When he became a professor, he found it shocking to encounter so many students who would receive inheritances. Their sense of self, and livelihood, depended on their achievements or how much material wealth they had. They became "slaves" to money, possession, and their minds. They were in a prison that they created for themselves.

After being exposed to this environment, he decided to quit his job at Yale. That experience led him to begin teaching others who had a passion for learning how to read or write but weren't raised in an environment conducive to allowing them to do so.

During his talk at my school, he was an influential figure in Latino literature and a powerful inspirational speaker.

A prison is not only a dark cage with bars—a prison can be an internal cage within one's mind. A cop on the outside of the bars can have metaphorical bars within the confines of his head. The man in the prison cell can cultivate mental freedom apart from his outer circumstance. He can become one of the world's most free men.

Riding the Wave

Do you know how to get out of a riptide (or rip current)? The people who never make it out alive are those who panic. Those who tire themselves out by fighting with a current they have *no chance* of influencing get overtaken by these momentary "storms."

Those who give up the fight, who do not panic and decide to flow with the current, are more likely to make it out alive after the "storm" has passed. It is like the trees that can bend in the wind, wherever it pushes them.

I had a real-life experience once, which demonstrated the need for surrender during an uncontrollable situation.

It was my dream to go on a hot air balloon ride for years. One day, I went online and bought the ticket; I called to make a reservation and set a date.

Hot air balloons use fire to heat the air inside the balloon; this causes it to become less dense than the air outside of the balloon—so it rises. As the balloon gets into the air, the pilot will add more heat to cause the balloon to raise or turn off the fire to lower the balloon. The rest depends on the wind currents; it's a *riding the wave* type of aircraft.

If wind conditions are not conducive to a safe ride, the pilot will stop the flight early or choose not to fly that day. On the day of our flight, the wind conditions were favorable. It seemed effortless to be floating up in the air. It's precisely how I would imagine flying (as a bird) would feel.

The only sounds we could hear were the voices of the other people in the aircraft, the gentle breeze, and the *whoosh* of the fire as the pilot heated the air inside of the balloon.

My eyes filled with tears as I delighted in that present moment, overlooking a scene of hills, trees, and the sun rising. After about 30-40 minutes, we began lowering towards the ground. The pilot explained that the wind conditions were starting to become unsafe.

We began lowering the aircraft for a safe landing. We lowered down towards a dirt road, right up against a barbed-wire fence. As we were landing, it became clear that we might not make it onto the ground without hitting the fence. The wind was pushing us closer to it.

Quietness filled the air as we prayed for our pilot to land us safely on the ground (without hitting the fence). We all held our breath as he landed *right* up against it without touching it.

One man, who was holding onto the side of the crate we were in, had to move his hand quickly, or it would've gotten cut by the fence. That was how close we were to it. Once we were safe on the ground, a man shouted jokingly, "Ow, my neck!" Everyone burst into laughter. It was just the comedic relief we all needed at that moment.

When we were lowering, a park ranger was standing on the other side of the gate we landed next to. The land that she was standing on was protected grounds. She shouted to our pilot that we could not pass over that gate because her side contained protected land.

Though we had already landed, the air balloon was massive. The balloon part had to be folded over the fence and placed on the ground (the protected land). Then once it was on the floor, the men could fold it, pack it up, and transport it back to the air balloon company's place of business.

The ranger explained that he should pick up the aircraft and move to a new spot so that we didn't cross over the gate. Our pilot told her:

If we pick up the balloon at all, the wind will push us into the fence, and much more damage will happen. We need to put tarps onto your side of the gate to lower the balloon part. We will pack up quickly, but I cannot move to a different spot.

He observed that the wind was beginning to pick up and knew that if he lifted the balloon from the ground at all, the wind would swiftly push us right through that fence, knock it over, and potentially hurt the people in the aircraft (us). Our best option was not to do what this ranger wanted him to do and instead, was to stay put right where we were.

So that he didn't put the people in the balloon in danger, the park ranger allowed the men to step over the gate, lower the balloon onto their side, and pack it up. Everyone safely got out of the hot air balloon and the only damage caused was to the sage bushes on the protected land.

This ranger had no choice but to allow us to crush these bushes momentarily, or the whole fence would be damaged (plus the aircraft and everyone in it would be entirely inside of the preserve, crushing the bushes anyways). The pilot, who skillfully understood how these balloons worked, made a calculated decision to avoid a much bigger (and potentially dangerous) mess than we were already in.

Sometimes in life, in the strong winds of external circumstance, surrendering is the wisest option. Acceptance, or non-resistance, within the storms of life is

Strength in Surrender

not *necessarily* an act of "giving up." It **is** an act of giving up the *internal struggle* of fighting with the outer circumstance. It's a choice to accept what is, knowing that "This too shall pass."

It is not a signal of defeat to raise a white flag and say, "I'm tired of fighting, I'm tired of struggling, I prefer happiness." It takes immense strength to recognize that sometimes it is wise to let life have its way with us; sometimes, we must put our hot air balloons onto the ground until it is safer to fly.

A friend recently asked me, in response to my beliefs on the subject, "If someone were stealing your car, would you just sit there and let them do it?" This argument seems, on the surface, to be a plausible rebuttal about why surrendering or inaction is unwise.

It is possible to act without making the other person an enemy that needs to be eradicated or punished for what they have done. Many people allow those situations to ruminate, which continues the problem within their minds (long after the situation has passed).

Internal struggle is also different than taking physical action that is necessary in a particular moment. It's like the man in the car who gets out to be in rain, instead of waiting for it to pass.

Mental surrender does not imply inaction. Guidance or intuition about the most effective action to take in any one situation is available when it's needed. A solution-oriented action is possible, whether that requires inaction or not, would be known at that time. Every case has many variables.

There can always be speculatory conversations about what one would do in any given situation. However, if I grew up in a completely different environment, was raised with entirely different ideals, and had seen a different world than the one I have been exposed to, I would respond to a situation much differently than in the current personality I identify with.

My teenage self would respond much differently to situations than my "current self." From one's state of viewing the world is where their actions originate. This is what I meant when I said that by transforming one's mental state, they transform their actions, lives, and therefore the world.

This is also where my compassion comes from, towards those who have taken harmful actions against strangers or their family members. They don't know better or cannot see how their actions have affected or *will affect* others.

When we look at a child or a dog, it is easy to conclude that *"they don't know any better."* When we see a human do something that we think they should not be doing, perhaps the more typical response would be, *"you should know better."*

This statement does not ask the questions of, where did this originate from? Why was that action taken? What situations led to that breaking point? What was their childhood environment like? What did they learn from the society around them? Did they have support systems or access to education about new philosophies and ideas? Did they have access to role models, and what did those role models teach them? Many factors build up a person's current identity, and therefore what they will cause in the world.

Bobcat in the Bushes

People who have experienced dangerous circumstances or experiences, have said that during a moment in which their life depended on a specific action, they just "knew" what to do. Or perhaps they "heard in their head" some guidance that saved their lives. This guidance comes out of presence. Life-threatening experiences force you to become aware of the present moment.

Writing about this reminds me of a time I was on a hike alone. As I walked, I thought to myself, "I wonder what I would do if a bobcat came out of the bushes." This thought came into my mind not fearfully or anxiously, but more like an internal question I was contemplating.

I thought, "I don't know what I would do if that were to happen. Perhaps in that split second, I would run, or use my metal water bottle as a weapon, or maybe I'd scream and yell (which would prompt someone to come and help me)."

I would know what to do at that moment *if* it were to happen. This is an example of action in response to a present moment threat. Taking the necessary present moment action is much different than allowing the fear of unknown factors to keep you from hiking.

If someone were stealing my car, I probably would do something—unless I knew intuitively, that it would be more dangerous than just letting them take it. It is all subjective to the situation.

The keyword here is "if" because this is one probability of many probable outcomes. I wouldn't let the tiny likelihood of a bobcat encounter, keep me from hiking. Perhaps on my hikes, I won't ever encounter a bobcat. Maybe if I did, it wouldn't even be interested in me.

Looking around for bobcats in bushes can lead to a life of never experiencing anything at all. The mind can very easily cause a person to become incapacitated. It can cripple them to the point of trapping themselves in a room for life (where they can never get hurt by a "bobcat"). It is not much different than being locked in a physical prison.

There are genuine threats in the world. The difference between looking for bobcats that *could possibly* come into your experience and being afraid because a bobcat is in front of you—are two completely different states of experiencing the world.

Honoring our fear, anger, and sadness, allowing the emotion to be acknowledged and moved through our body as it is—not running from, hiding from, numbing, or suppressing, is how we can live our lives freely.

Seeing the coping mechanisms, honoring them for saving us at one point in our lives, and then deciding to do it differently now that we have new resources and awareness is where healing and shifts in consciousness begin. It is where a change in the world begins.

Surrendering when we cannot control something, bending with wind when it comes, and understanding the constant nature of change that this reality implies, leads to a much easier life. Yet if you'd like to be the man yelling at the rain, that is always a choice too.

Chapter 6

The World Goes Blind

When the latest *Joker* movie[1] (starring Joaquin Phoenix) came out in theatres, a friend recommended that I see it, so I did. It follows how DC's "The Joker" became a "villain" in the Batman movies or comics.

It depicts his upbringing by a mentally ill mother. The audience sees all the times that he was disempowered, beaten down, judged, or pushed around by the people around him.

This movie demonstrates how he tries to find help externally, to ease his internal suffering. We watch as he helplessly visits psychiatrists, takes medications, searches for meaning and purpose in work, and reaches out for connection from the people around him. He eventually grows tired of being the ostracized, unwanted one.

He becomes disillusioned as society pushes him away, which in turn creates an intense pain within him. Like Baca, this was a man brought up by a cruel world. When he reaches his wit's end, when the pain of not belonging becomes unbearable, he gives up reaching out for love and takes control by becoming a "monster."

Out of his grief, he begins killing those who disempowered and abused him (including his mother). The world (of this movie) sees his gruesome actions on broadcasts and the news.

Again, but now in the public eye, he is the villain, ostracized for the things he's done. He is pushed away by society because all they can see in him is his "monstrous" tendencies, not the life which led him there. These people know nothing about him; they only judge him by his actions after he gives in to his rage.

They cannot see that these are the actions of someone who has only known a world of ostracization. Thus, a "villain" was birthed—a man pushed around, beaten into feeling like he had no choice other than to act on his pain and cause pain to others.

In starting a movement (no matter how "twisted" it appeared), the Joker finds solace in belonging somewhere, finally being seen and heard.

There's a "Log" in my Eye

Villains of the world are widely misunderstood. They are a product of the teachings of their ancestors, societies, and sometimes even religions. At a certain level, a victim can be found in all humans. They can be seen as a victim to their upbringings, genetics, societal structures already in place before they were born, the actions and decisions of their forefathers, and in some cases—the lack of support or connection they received.

A "guilty" aspect can also be found in all humans (at varying degrees). When you step on a flower, when you consume an animal product, even when you drive a car, you are causing harm to something or someone else.

There is no way around not causing some degree of harm in the world. I like to contemplate situations in this manner, all are guilty, and all are innocent. There are many sides, perspectives, situations, and many prior steps (or decisions) that lead someone to take a particular action.

Many others have said that "Hurt people hurt people." Abusers are those who were abused. When looked at from afar, seeing how these people have become the "monsters" that they are, compassion for the harmful actions of others comes easily. The "judgers" are acting out of their pain, too.

While studying Family Constellations, I've learned much about war and the origin of harmful acts. My understanding (up to this point) is that harmful actions are committed out of innocence.

What I mean is that if someone goes to war, they are often doing so out of love for their "country" or their "people." The people on the other end are fighting back for the very same reasons.

They are both doing so with blind love. Because they have killed, they gave life to those who came after them. I would not be alive if it were not for all the decisions that have come before me in my ancestry. It was a butterfly effect that led to my specific existence, and yours.

I have noticed in our society that we see justice as "An eye for an eye." It appears many believe that to cause change, one must make the playing field even.

Cancel culture is an excellent example of collective ostracization to control one's behavior. It says, "You did something horrible; now we will repay you by ruining your life, because we are the right and innocent ones." This denies their own guiltiness in the world and is a sort of righteousness that says, "I have been better than you, and know better, so you need to be punished for what you did."

Sometimes companies will not work with the "canceled" individual—even if they were wrongly accused. It would be bad for business. With the threat of losing their livelihood, acceptance within a group, or good reputation, it makes sense how powerful this can be to control another person's actions. When we are afraid of consequences, we are more likely not to do something or to do it in secret when others are not watching. An excellent example of this is a teenager whose parents won't allow him to go out to a party, so he instead hides the fact that he will go to a party by telling them he's going to his friend's house for the night.

This human tendency also makes it glaringly evident just how accustomed to controlling another's actioning, many people have become. A seemingly benign example of this would be, "I will leave a horrible review so that people won't support you anymore, and I can ruin your business."

We can also see this in how much pressure "celebrities" are under. They must tiptoe around their words and actions, lest the paparazzi catch something that could get them canceled.

This reactionary response (of revenge) never once questions why these "wrong ones" are this way, nor how they became the "villains" that we currently see them as. These are the "rejects," the "unacceptable," the "unlovable," because of one's inability to have compassion or love for another's scars and wounds. It also originates from their failure to see their own faults.

These "justice seekers" are also unaware that by villainizing these "others," they have also become "villains" themselves. If an "accuser" (someone who deems someone else as unacceptable because of their actions) has decided they should put the "perpetrator" to death for what they have done, are they both now "accusable?"

The two parties harm one another, and each feels as if they are justified in their actions to keep passing pain. The two parties go to war out of innocent love for their side but don't question what it would be like to be on the other end. If they lived that life exactly how the wrongdoer lived it, perhaps they could have become exactly as they are.

In this state, there is no love, no compassion for the other, and no attempt to understand what has led this person to this point of becoming like "The Joker" villain or the "Frankenstein."

It would be immensely effective to give love, compassion, and understanding to those who need it the most (the people in the most pain). It is much easier said than done when someone is standing in your face shouting at you, but it is possible.

If we look at Jimmy Santiago Baca again, we see this imprisoned man, a man who grew up in a situation that led to unconscious patterns that hurt many others. Perhaps he would be seen as a "monster" in that state. People do not condemn him now because of his own choice to "redeem" himself (become a "better" person). Now he is looked up to, by many, and is seen as an inspiration.

I am not saying that it is all right or justified to take your pain out on others. I am trying to illustrate that the world is simply not so "black" and "white." Again, one's view of rightness and wrongness stems from their environment, the opinions of whoever has surrounded them since their birth.

When someone is yelling in your face, or when it's coming from someone important in your life, it is not always so easy to find compassion. Like that saying, "Easier said than done."

We often face others who are in a bad mood because of whatever has happened in their lives (and are taking unconscious action out of this state of mind).

Everyone who has experienced massive amounts of depression, anger, or grief, knows that when we are amidst that type of pain—anyone who unwittingly steps onto our path, had better run the other way. That is why the saying of "being blinded by rage" or "seeing red," is so well-known.

The being experiencing this state of mind is in one of pain, so anyone who steps into their field is looked at through the eyes of whatever they are experiencing (whether it be anger, resentment, pain, etc.)

A Story of Forgiveness

"I blame the devil, who misguided and led you to do such a horrible crime, and I forgive you." A Muslim man named Abdul-Munim Sombat Jitmoud[3] said these words in court as he looked his son's murderer in the eyes. His 22-year-old son was robbed and killed, an act which could not be reversed.

All in the courtroom were moved to tears when they witnessed this man's ability to forgive the hurt that a young man caused to another (his son). This story demonstrates the transformative power of surrender and forgiveness in a situation where many people would find it tremendously hard to do so.

It shows how one man decided to release the pain of having lost something invaluable to him. He became a testament to the change possible with love, to all who were in that room, and to his son's killer especially. A dark situation created a crack of light, for this man to help many other people to choose different actions and not to cause more harm in the world.

There is footage of this father and this murderer hugging. The one who killed, through apologetic tears, said, "I can't do anything to give him back to you."

Through this father's pardoning of this man's "sin," he opened the doorway to remorse and change within this young man's life. Imagine what kind of change that can cause in another's life.

When you can look at them with love, seeing the pain they have caused in your life or others', and say, "I can see what led you to become that, and I know you can, and will, do better."

We cannot undo the past. Resentment towards others' misdeeds only continues the cycle of pain. It breeds unhappiness, divides people, and can make you sick.

Forgiveness sets all free—not only the "perpetrators" but also the "victims" because, again, *all* are victims to their environments, desires, and humanness.

"Punishment" out of Pain: An Experience

While I was working at the metaphysical shop I mentioned at the beginning of this book, I had an experience with a customer that I think is relevant to this topic.

During the holidays (around Christmas time), a woman came to me asking for help to choose a gift for one of her family members. It began as a pleasant interaction, she decided what she would like, and as I started ringing her up for her items, she handed me a gift card for the mall (as her payment).

I tried to swipe this card into our system, but it was not working. It wasn't until after I tried to swipe it, and it wasn't working, that I realized we couldn't take that payment.

After I called the mall management to fix the issue, I found out that it was because we were an independent business. I let the woman know that I could not take that form of payment and why it was not possible.

Her face went red, and with rage in her eyes, she began yelling at me. It was apparent that she felt utterly powerless to her pain—her emotions overtook her.

Through gritted teeth, she explained to me what was happening in her life, the people who were hurting her, the health issues she was experiencing, her recent loss of a family member—all intending to get me to do what she wanted me to do.

Though I wanted to make it work for her, there was nothing I could do. I explained that I was sorry that her life was so difficult, but I couldn't take the payment even if I wanted to.

In an "eye for an eye" manner, she began threatening me out of her pain, to influence the situation. She told me she would call the mall management over to have them "straighten me out."

She demanded the owner's information so that she could get me fired. I handed her my boss's business card, apologized, and again explained that I still could not take the payment. She stormed off.

If I fought back with her (or took it personally) and decided that since she was hurting me, I should hurt her back, this unconscious cycle of pain could have continued. We could have ended up both sitting there defeated, even angrier, and with even more pain than when we started.

This was a small and benign example of the destruction that acting out of one's pain can cause. There are instances of far more insidious destruction that this form of pain-induced action can cause in the world.

This "Eye for an eye, you hurt me so I hurt you," form of payback can become a vicious cycle of pain—that is, until one person decides to create a small opening of awareness. Just one person can decide to step away from suffering, not internalize the others' pain, and pardon the actions they have taken out of their "unconsciousness."

True justice or change starts here, with one person choosing to bring more awareness into a situation. The difference is not just within that relationship; it happens within all who encounter the being who has become more conscious of their reactions and emotions.

The person who chooses not to act out of painful or unconscious emotion causes ripples of change with all who he encounters.

As I said previously, surrendering is not an act of weakness or defeat. This also does not imply denying, disowning, or suppressing these darker emotions. Working through those emotions, experiencing, and understanding where they come from and not taking it out on someone else, is an act of love for the self and the other.

It is a conscious choice not to contribute to the unconsciousness or pain of the world. To not contribute to the cycle of pain, that is, "You hurt me, so I hurt you, and now she hurt me, so I'll keep passing it on."

Imagine what that butterfly effect looks like on a much larger scale. If it mattered to me that this woman was so mean, or if I internalized it (was drawn into the pain with her), then it would have been easy to keep passing pain. If I allowed it to affect my emotional world, it could have tainted my interactions with every customer after her.

Then there is the possibility for my interactions with other customers to bleed into their interactions with others (and their interactions with the people they meet, and on and on).

All those painful interactions stemmed from this one interaction I had with one woman who was in massive amounts of pain because of how her life was going. If she had a larger view than only her perspective, if she knew how powerless I was to change the situation, compassion would be the response, not revenge.

Yet still, even in causing pain to another, it's like the boy with the horse I wrote about earlier in this book. Good can lead to bad, and bad can lead to good. Having that experience with that woman has led to you reading this story and hopefully being inspired to change. Bad to good, good to bad.

I am not suggesting that people should allow themselves to be abused or mistreated. This sounds like a state of disempowerment—allowing others to walk all over you.

That is not the case; boundaries can be voiced and enforced with love for oneself and another. You can say no to what you feel is not okay or remove yourself from a situation without making an enemy out of whoever has caused pain. All situations are individual, have many factors. Generalizations within *any* teaching cannot give answers to every situation for every person on the planet.

When I went onto my journey and began learning from the strangers I encountered, the lesson I learned through that experience, was that there are an infinite amount of sides to one story. People say this all the time within relationships, that it's important to consider that each person has their perspective.

They will view the world through the lens that they have. Two people looking at the same painting will see two different paintings; they will have their own opinions, and responses to that exact one. The painting is still only a painting; the individual human's way of seeing this painting, though, is his responsibility. It's his free choice whether he sees its beauty or its imperfections. It's his choice if he is offended by it, wants to tear it off the wall, or wants to appreciate the masterpiece that someone took their time to create.

This is the case for each individual's view on things like religion, morality, the right way to do something, or "goodness" and "badness." With the opportunity and openness to choose to learn why some people view things a certain way, perhaps this is where it is possible to eradicate the possibility of hurting another human being. Knowing what it is like to hurt and where somebody came from, breeds compassion, forgiveness, and understanding.

When you know what someone's family is like, what it was like to walk in their shoes, and how they became who they are, hurting them would cause you pain yourself. I once heard a spiritual teacher liken this idea to fingers of the same hand. Each finger is still individual, apart from the body, yet if you hurt one of them, you are still hurting yourself. Each is connected, and each of them is part of you.

All individual humans are part of the whole. All actions create effects in the world. Like Baca came to discover—words can heal or cause more harm. A choice that **you** make can change someone's life, for better or for worse.

CHAPTER 7

Perfection is Non-Existent, Diversity is Constant

For seventh grade (and part of eighth), I went to a school for children and teens who desired to become firefighters or police officers. I decided to join this school because my best friends (ones I grew up with throughout elementary) were transferring there. I wanted to stick with them.

This school was essentially a "military school." We wore combat boots, uniforms that looked like police officer outfits, and caps with our last names. The girls' hair had to be put up into buns, while the males had to be clean-shaven (no long hair). Girls could not have colorful hair or wear any makeup that made them stand out as "different from the others."

Every morning, we began our day by standing in "formation." We had our designated spots with varying levels of importance. The sergeants stood up front overseeing us; then we had corporals who each stood at the beginning of our line to lead us "cadets."

The school's built-in system instructed these "leaders" to ensure we all complied with the rules. The adults of the school, applauded them for making sure that we did not talk to our friends or "step out of line."

It was like a chain of commanders making sure their subordinates did as they said because *all* were in the unconscious (or conscious) fear of those above them. There was the fear of punishment by ostracization, physical harm through "exercise," or the disappointment of not being a good leader in the eyes of their "commanders" or "chiefs."

If we were not listening to the teacher, or if one person was "acting out," the teacher would stop our lecture and send us outside for what was called intensive training (I.T.). All students would get in a line, run down the stairs of the back door of the building, and prepare for whatever the teacher had in store for us.

Sometimes we would do "Indian runs," where we all ran in a single-file line, and the last person in line would run to the front of the line. This would continue until the very first person it began with got back to the front. We would also have to hold our arms up to do butterfly circles for long periods, as the teacher watched over us with a timer. If one person put their arms down out of pain or exhaustion, the timer would restart, and everyone would hate that person for making us all start over with them. We would be forced to push our every limit. Even if our bodies were crying out to put our arms down, we had to keep them up or else start all over.

At other times, the teacher would have us do sit-ups or stand in a squat position until our legs were shaking.

The cause of having to endure these exercises varied. Sometimes, it would be because a student was talking during a lecture or wasn't listening to the teacher. We would all "pay" for what that student did.

I would imagine the adults wanted to teach us to work together, consider each other's well-being, and form camaraderie with our peers. It is a sort of selflessness to "behave" so that your teammates don't get in trouble with you. However, the flip side of that coin was that it also taught the children not to be different. It taught them to fear the consequences of not doing what the adult thought we should be doing (or wanted us to do).

If one dares to be different, like acting out, or not wearing a uniform correctly, the punishment factor effectively trains people not to take that action. They would be too afraid of the repercussions (and so choose not to do it).

This "group creating" happens at varying levels among many groups of people. When one group differs from another, it can breed intolerance for the "others" who have diverse viewpoints, thoughts, opinions, backgrounds, habits, or cultures.

In that school, there were groups of corporals, sergeants, and cadets. Each had different tasks and different levels of importance. The subordinates were to look to their leaders for direction and instruction.

A position like that can teach people much about leadership; I'm not saying it's all bad (nothing is all good or bad, remember). However, it can also teach those leaders to become intolerant of variances in personality, preference, or need, among incredibly diverse human beings.

We came from different backgrounds and were raised by various parents (like the seedlings in different environments). Yet when we went to school, most of us, were "cadets" in identical uniforms, in identities that we had to wear when we got to school—or else get into trouble.

The Origin of Judgment

With this school's story in mind, I want to dive a bit deeper into the origin of judgment, and how love, or belonging to a group, can be what causes someone to harm another.

Diversion from the accepted norm within a group threatens uniformity—those who identify with the group, long to belong. Depending on how strong their tie to this belonging is, they could become enemies with anyone who threatens that belonging.

Humans are driven by connection. Belonging with others, or to a particular group of ideas or beliefs, creates a state of innocence and connectedness (as previously stated in the last chapter).

It can be something as simple as, "my family puts the aluminum cans in the recycle trash" vs. "my family puts them in the regular trash." If two people marry each other—who belong to opposite families—well, you can see how this could bring about many arguments if they decide to hang onto what they "belong to." Every time one sees a can in the wrong trash, their origin of belonging is threatened.

Thus, "enemies" are those who threaten the groups we belong to. All places of belonging, essentially, stem from love. It is like the belief of, "I love my people, so I will go to war for them, to protect them." They see themselves as the right group and cannot open to the possibility of a new perspective. That is how strong of a tie their love to *their* group can bind someone to their beliefs.

Many fights, big or small, come from making an enemy out of someone who threatens one's sense of belonging. Both sides want to belong in their group; both sides believe that they are justified in fighting for their belief, and acts that can cause much suffering and pain can manifest.

What someone belongs to can be completely unconscious to themselves. Whenever they feel resistance while listening to a differing opinion than their own—that is when their "group of belonging" is revealed.

For example, say you hear someone claim, "I don't think people of the same sex should get married because it is a sin."

When the emotional response of defensiveness or anger arises—this reveals that you "belong" with the group that believes others should have the freedom to love who they want to.

My point is not to decide who is correct or not—I desire to show that both sides see themselves as the right one because someone taught them it was "good." They came to those views out of childlike love, out of the need to belong in the groups they were born into (or decided to choose in their lives).

For the person who believes it is a sin, this may be the underlying belief:

> My religion believes that same-sex marriage is a sin. Doing so, would mean that I, or anyone who does that, will suffer in hell.

This view, when looked at objectively (not as right or wrong), can be seen this way:

I love my religion, I love the family I belong to (who are part of that religion), and I love you; I don't want you to go to hell—so I have to do my best to make sure you don't commit those "sins."

It is an innocent and unconscious love—the rightness or wrongness of this view in our own awareness, depends on what groups we belong to.

I was once called the word "brain-washed" by someone who had strong beliefs about religion. When I began my spiritual explorations, which were against their Christian beliefs, they didn't want their ideas to be challenged.

I concluded that if they traveled or were open to exploring differing opinions, they would come to understand another's experience. If they "walked in someone else's shoes" or learned about new people, then they would see why those people have come to their conclusions, biases, judgments, and preferences.

We have no control over the beliefs or actions of another human being, as these choices come from their point of viewing the world. As shown in the example of the people in Plato's cave allegory, the only reality we can ever know is solely derived from what we have experienced.

A man named Donald Rumsfeld once said:

There are known knowns...things we know we know...there are known unknowns...we know there are some things we don't know... there are unknown unknowns—the ones we don't know we don't know.[1]

We cannot know what we have never experienced or encountered. When someone goes against what a large group of people have agreed is the right way, he can face massive amounts of backlash. Even if this way is a better way, the group can have deeply tied attachments to that way of being, and so make an enemy of that outlier.

Many people in history who stepped out of the societal "norm" or "box" were ostracized for their differing opinions. Others sometimes disowned them, because they were an anomaly within what a group of people believed was good or right.

Being "different" from another human being is a beautiful facet of life experience. Jesus, Muhammed, Gandhi, Martin Luther King Jr., and Rosa Parks received much backlash when they wished to create what they saw as a positive change.

These people were not afraid to step out of a societal "norm," not afraid to stand up for what they knew in their hearts was truest to themselves and what they felt was right.

Even some scientific leaders who were not afraid to look past what they were taught (like Tesla, Albert Einstein, and Charles Darwin) were seen as crazy for looking at a new perspective that people were not yet ready to accept.

Perfection is Non-Existent, Diversity is Constant

Diversity gives rise to new opinions and the further development of perspectives. New inventions arise out of this openness. If no one ever challenged old systems, religions, inventions, or philosophies, people could never improve upon them.

If this natural evolvement didn't happen, you and I would not be looking at cell phone screens. We wouldn't be able to call others on the phone, and there would be no such thing as light bulbs or light.

If we go far back enough, at the beginning of humankind, if they had not explored new possibilities, there would be no fire, no societies, perhaps no language or sophisticated ways of communicating, and no improved ways of trade. The list is massive. New frontiers are where evolution comes from.

I try not to turn down ideas that differ from mine. This openness has allowed me to witness the many "otherworldly" experiences I have had thus far.

I believe it is a Zen philosophy to keep an "Is that so?" mind, or a "Maybe" mind. Maybe it is true, and perhaps it is not true. Maybe someone's perception is correct for them, but that does not mean it has to be correct for you.

Maybe your specific view of a painting can generate a more pleasurable way of existing on earth than the way they are teaching you that you should look at that painting.

Perfection is Non-Existent

When I began learning how to drive, I was *terrified* to drive on freeways. I would purposefully look up routes to go only on streets that had stoplights.

My fear stemmed from how fast everyone was going on the freeway. I found it petrifying to try and merge with other cars that were going *70* to *80* miles per hour.

In my mind, that was lightning speed. I had to press hard on the gas to get my car to reach the same pace. I felt like a race car driver, trying to keep up with these "crazy folk!"

At the beginning of learning how to drive, I was in the turning lane to turn left at a stoplight, to go into a parking lot. The stoplight didn't have a "turn on the green arrow" light—it was a yield to the oncoming traffic light. I didn't know this intuitively at the time, so when it turned green, I thought it was my turn to go, and I went. I almost caused a massive accident.

After turning into this parking lot, I parked and sat in panic. "I should go home," I thought.

I think of this experience whenever I'm hard on myself for getting something wrong. I was simply learning something brand new. I didn't know the rules of the road. If, on that day, I got discouraged and decided, "Nope, driving is not for me," I would never have gotten better at it.

Years later, driving has become like second nature to me. It's something I don't even think about. I merge onto freeways seamlessly; my car became like an extension of me. I understand how fast it can speed up and how quickly it can slow down. "Mastery" developed through being behind the wheel, many times, in many places.

The skill developed *because* of messing up. It developed *because* of each time that I chose to get back into the car and behind the wheel.

Nobody is ever an expert the first time they do something—no matter what it is. Mastery comes with time and practice. Just as these innovative thinkers didn't shy away from looking at how something could be improved upon, they also had the understanding that nothing is, or will ever be, perfect.

Self-Worth and "Beauty"

Your ancestors made many choices; countless mothers and fathers have said yes to each other, to manifest *you* specifically, to be here in this moment, *as* you are, *wherever* you are, *however* you are.

Much of the discomfort associated with insecurity, is derived from comparing the self with what others have or look like. It is cultivated by a society that denies its natural tendency to evolve, grow, mature, and (eventually) return to the source from which it came.

There is a confidence that goes beyond form, beyond one's appearance, beyond one's belongings, beyond one's status within a company, beyond all physical conditions. Perhaps confidence is not the best word to use here. Maybe love and an understanding of the nature of our reality, is a better way to describe it. In this view, there is an inherent detachment to one's physical beauty, as it is not "who *they* are."

There is nothing wrong with enjoying our physical bodies and looks (while we have them). If we become attached to that form or what it brings to us from others (be it compliments, adoration, or "likes"), it will eventually cause massive amounts of pain and suffering as we get old or sick. "I got a pimple, oh no!" "Is that grey hair? My life is over!"

Have you ever looked at a baby and thought, "That baby is way too chubby. She needs to go running and stop eating sweets, to get rid of some of those baby fat rolls"?

I never have, but that baby has *never* looked into a mirror and thought to themselves those kinds of thoughts, at least not to my knowledge (maybe we should ask a baby).

They have not yet learned from the world what the standard of "beauty" is. The child has not yet begun to compare their looks, belongings, or status, to what others say is best, right, or good. They have not yet been through schooling, have not been told by parents how they ought to act. They simply are what they are. They cry when they need something, scream if they don't like something—even if that's in the middle of a grocery store. They aren't yet afraid that they will be judged for throwing a tantrum. They don't stuff, hold, or suppress their pain; when they feel it, *everybody* knows.

A duck never tells another duck that its feathers are the wrong color, that instead of being black, it should be white. A fly doesn't say to another fly that its wings are not fast enough.

A bear isn't worried about the extra belly fat gained over the winter while hibernating. I've never seen a butterfly take a selfie, post it, and wait for the comments to come in from others about how beautiful she is!

The age of social media has catapulted many to grow up in a world where the lives of others are even more glaringly at their fingertips. That can give rise to an even more prominent feeling of inadequacy than one might have felt before social media was invented. Before, maybe it was more like, "My next-door neighbor Suzie makes much better food than I ever could."

Now, people have access to the inside scoop of thousands or millions of lives. One can now see the riches that many famous people have amassed and see the lifestyles they live.

This state of comparing can also be passed to children by parents who have insecurities because of their lives before having children. Many have learned to look externally for self-validation and a sense of worthiness.

Beauty is in the eye of the beholder, and if the one beholding you is insecure or has a lack of self-love (because of what others taught them), they will have no access to appreciating your "beauty."

Someone's evaluation of you solely has to do with their state of mind (their learned views, judgments, environment, whatever they are going through). It is not an indicator of your rightness, your worthiness, or your value.

My Family Constellation teacher once taught me,

I can make food, place it on the table for others to come and eat if they want to. I cannot force them to eat it, but they can take it if they'd like to. If they don't, they can go to someone else's table or make their own food. What they choose is none of my business. It is best to do things *with* love, not *for* love.

Authenticity

Authenticity can be interpreted in many ways, depending on who the interpreter is, their perspective, and the specific situation we consider.

In my experience, I have found that being authentic within our human experience is not always easy. As previously stated, from the moment that we are born, we are not "lovable" if we do something that makes someone angry or uncomfortable. When we are children, if we talk when the teacher is lecturing, the consequence is,

"Get out of the class or go to the principal so they can deal with you."

The message this can bring to the child is, "If I don't conform, I will be unloved, and it means I am not good enough, so I must always do as they say." At varying degrees, there is an inherent people-pleaser in every human being alive in our current societal structures. This leads to adults whose lives were lived for other people. It develops into a world of people who became doctors because their families told them to do it, but who live and die extremely unhappy.

It can feel like doing something "wrong" to choose authenticity in each moment. When faced with someone else's opinion, I ask myself, "Do I want to live the life others want for me? Or do I want to live the life I want for me?"

Forsaking your preferences and choices leads to resentment towards the one who told you what to do. It's easy to say, "You got me into this mess; I didn't even want this for myself." Yet, we are the ones that choose to let others decide for us.

I would define authenticity as the choice to live for yourself. As we grow into adulthood, our healing and our lives are entirely in our own hands. There is no more, "But my parents did or didn't do something, or I wasn't given the opportunity to." We can pave our way; we can create our opportunities. We can change the beliefs and the patterns of those who came before us.

Authenticity includes saying something you feel needs to be said in a particular moment, following your passions, and wearing what you want. Not what you think will look appealing to someone else.

It is the choice to be okay with being the "outcasted" one within specific groups. Because with this authentic self on the table, you can attract the types of people you would like to be surrounded by. Those people will like you for you, not for a mask you're putting on.

Dancing for Yourself

As a young child (around four or five years old), I loved dancing. My parents had a T.V., which had many channels with multiple genres of music—it ranged anywhere from rap, to hip-hop, to jazz, to classical, to rock, or to pop. I loved putting on "shows."

My joy did not come from them liking my dance—it came from the pure joy of dancing. I would jump up onto the fireplace, become a ballerina when the classical music came on, and when they'd switch the channel to jazz, I would transform into a tap dancer! Rap would come on, and now I was a hip-hop dancer.

I never once thought, "Oh no, they are not going to like this type of dance. They will think I look like a complete idiot! I should sit down and never dance again!" I wasn't yet conditioned by adults or society to "look nice for others."

Somewhere in my life, I learned not to be so "weird." I subconsciously took on social cues to fit in because of the fear of ostracization. It sounds like my school, doesn't it?

I stopped deciding to dance as I grew older. I decided that it might be better not to stand up or look weird. That would keep me safe from the unhappy bullies. Perhaps that would keep me safe from others who might tell me I should sit back down with them to keep them company. Or maybe it would save me from being looked at with judgmental eyes by an audience.

It wasn't until my adulthood, during an unexpected circumstance with a stranger, that I recognized how afraid and controlled I became because of the fear of others' judgments.

When I was on the Abraham Hicks cruise to Alaska, one night was dedicated for all members to get together for a cocktail party. I was sitting alone listening to the music at this party when a woman walked up to me.

She began a conversation, asking what I did for work. We talked about how we ended up on that ship to be standing there together. She then asked me, "Do you want to dance?"

I looked at her shockingly, as if she had just asked me to jump off a bridge with her. "No, absolutely not."

"Why not?"

"Because I don't like to dance for other people," I said assuredly.

"Then why don't you dance for yourself?"

I sat in my chair, looking at the wall across from me as I thought to myself. She was so right. Why should I sit there afraid of what people would think of me for getting up? Why should I stifle my fun so that I could feel comfortable in my seat?

It made no sense to allow others' opinions to keep me from dancing. That was the opposite of freedom. That was enslavement to the opinions of another. That was like allowing their viewpoints to be the rope that tied up my wings.

At first, when we got up, I felt a bit awkward, as if I didn't want to fully "unleash the beast." Then a song by Whitney Houston came on. We both got excited. I looked at her and said, "I love this song!" We began singing every word to each other. It was like singing to myself in a mirror.

Suddenly, I didn't care what anyone thought about my dancing—hell, I didn't even care if I looked like an idiot. I channeled my inner diva, my inner Beyonce. I just wanted to be free and to have unabashed, uninhibited fun on the dance floor. Not the "sexy" kind of looking good for others. The *beast* was unleashed.

We danced for a while together, until she told me she had to leave because she needed to find her friend. I told her to go ahead and go and that I would stay on the dance floor—it was too much fun to stop. I "danced like nobody was watching," *all by myself*.

In that state of pure bliss, it felt like it didn't matter if anyone was watching. I knew I would never see those people ever again.

People were coming up to me and asking to dance with me because it "looked like I was having so much fun." The singer up on the stage was giggling because my joy was just infectious! That or I looked like an idiot. Either way, I was having so much fun (like a little kid).

This experience taught me much about authenticity. Children are lovely examples of this—they will get up and dance their hearts out for *fun*.

When we choose to get up and dance among a group of people who have learned not to stand out, the response from the crowd is not always positive. I would rather be the one up and dancing than the one sitting down critiquing her dance.

Perhaps encountering someone whose wings don't have ropes tied around them, will inspire them to cut their own ropes that tie them up.

Chapter 8

Giving and Receiving

Imagine two people standing on either side of a pipe—if one person closes off their side, they cannot give to the other. They also cannot receive. This shuts off both from experiencing the connection of love that would be possible if their pipes were open.

Think of an ape caring for its brother by picking out the bugs in his hair—this ape doesn't think to itself, "I will pick your bugs so that I will be more worthy in your eyes, and you will do more things for me." One can speculate that it is a selfless act of love.

In-kind, this ape will have his bugs picked out of his hair eventually—but he will not be waiting for the other to do it because he expects repayment. It is not a transaction that subconsciously has strings attached to it.

Now, picture someone giving a gift to another, but they have strings attached to the box they're holding onto as they hand it over to the other person. The other person says, "Wow, thank you so much!" Days later, the one who received the gift accidentally hurts the giver's feelings.

The giver of the gift knows, "Hey, I have strings attached to the gift I gave you; I'll just pull them back or let you know I have the strings, so you know not to hurt me!" What this is, is a way to hold something over the others' head. It's a gift that they gave conditionally—not really a "gift" at all.

Now, whenever the giver tries to give a gift in the future, the other will not want to take it for fear of it being taken back. Trust was breached before, so the underlying feeling of the receiver would go something like this:

> How can I know you will not hold this over my head if I unintentionally hurt your feelings? Is it *actually* a gift, or are you trying to have something to hold over my head to get me to do what you want me to do?

So, what would cause someone to give gifts that have strings? It is not intentional; we often don't know that we have tied strings to our gifts *until* the person hurts us and we want to take the gift back.

The reason for strings could stem from a wounded inner-child. It is essentially, having the pipe closed for fear of the person on the other side taking advantage of your "kindness." It's like looking through the pipe, shouting, "Hey, where's the reciprocation? I just pushed some love your way; where's mine?"

This wound could stem from childhood relationships with parents or friends. A good example is a child who was given the role of caretaker within the family. Others took so much from them that they eventually felt like everyone was taking *too much* from them. They grow up looking through pipes whenever they get into friendships or relationships.

What would cause a person to "close off their pipe?" Often, this is a subconscious or unconscious pattern that one cannot see about themselves—until they see it.

When children grow up with a caretaker who cannot fulfill their needs (or give love), they turn inwards. It can also be called an "interrupted movement of the soul." When a child reaches outwards and is rejected repeatedly, they will stop reaching out and internalize the pain within. They will shut themselves off from receiving anything so that they won't have to feel the discomfort of this unbearable loss.

It is an unconscious attempt to regain control over something that caused emotional harm. This withdrawal is a coping mechanism to handle the pain of disconnectedness.

Picture a child who puts a large brick wall in between themselves and all others. Even though they long to connect with others, it is much safer to keep this wall up. When she grows up, people on the other side begin throwing paper notes to her, asking that she let her walls down so they can come in. Yet, by the time she's an adult, she's so used to having these walls and being "alone" that she isn't even conscious of these walls existing.

The inner child is giving love freely, but it keeps hitting a wall, never reaching the other side for others to feel it. Her wall developed as a coping mechanism to keep her safe from the world.

So, her adult self concludes that it's everyone else who doesn't want to connect with her. What's happening is that she doesn't have an open pipe to receive from others. They couldn't give even if they wanted to because she is the one not open to receiving. No matter what anyone tries to give, it will never be enough because it is her own "hole," so to speak.

Giving everything to another and never taking (unconsciously) allows one to maintain a state of power over another. To some, it is seemingly "admirable" to be self-sufficient and not need from others. It can actually be like saying to the other person, "I see you're incapable, and I am more capable because I have more than you, so out of my pity, I will give to you and not ask for anything back."

Giving and Receiving

It causes the recipient to remain indebted to the giver—because now the giver can bring it up that they have done so much, and so you "owe" them for all those times that they gave to you. This is a subconscious way to protect the inner child from getting hurt. It's like telling the child, "I will fend for you; I've already got a plan to take them down if they hurt us." All the child wants to do, is to love freely.

On the flip side, taking and never giving is also an unhealthy energetic bond that binds one to another. This taker becomes indebted to the one who gives him everything.

They are like a baby bird whose mother chews his food and feeds it to him; it stunts his growth and never allows him the opportunity to fly from his nest. It is like slavery that takes away their ability to provide for or love another. It is a different form of "having the pipe closed." It is like, "I take so much and don't flow it back to the other."

A taker and a giver are a perfect match for each person's wounded inner child. The giver gets to remain in protective mode, and the taker keeps his love to himself so as not to get hurt by someone who's not willing to receive it. Neither has to do the work to heal their inner wounds.

In love (platonic acquaintances, romantic partnerships, familial relationships, friendships, etc.), there is an equal giving and taking necessary for love to flow effectively, harmoniously, and freely.

Close yourself off to receiving from others, and you have closed off to receiving love. Close yourself off to giving, and you have closed yourself off to experiencing what it is like to allow love to flow through you to another.

This topic reminds me of a particular experience I had with a homeless woman a few years back. I was sitting outside a coffee shop, reading a book, when a woman came up to me. She said, "Hi, I'm sorry I don't mean to bug you, but I wanted to ask if you could please buy me a pizza from the place next door."

"Yes, let's go."

As we walked, she began telling me what she would like on her slice of pizza. I said, "Why don't you come inside with me and order?"

It hadn't occurred to her that she was allowed to come inside with me. We walked in, and I told her she could tell the pizza maker what she wanted. He made her food, we walked out together, and I told her to sit with me while she ate.

She told me how she became homeless, where she usually slept, and we talked about our spiritual beliefs. She noticed that the book I was reading was spiritual.

After she finished her food, she thanked me for sitting with her and buying her food. Then she went on her way. She gave me more that day than I gave to her when I decided to buy her a pizza. Her choice to be open to receiving opened the door for me to know the joy of giving.

My heart filled with so much gratitude for the moment she provided for me. It was eye-opening to hear a story from a woman whose life had been much different than my own. I gained an understanding of her life, and got to experience her appreciation for receiving a small gift that I could provide.

Her joy was the repayment—"I will pick your bugs, and you don't have to pick mine back."

Love says, "I see you have bugs on your back. I will get them for you, and when you see some bugs on my back, you can get them for me. I won't hold it against you if you don't; you don't owe me anything." Figuratively speaking, of course. If I have an actual bug on my back, seriously, please get it.

Open to Receiving: An Experience

In chapter two, I talked a bit about my experience with the Soka Gakkai Buddhists. The first time that I met them, they taught me about the objects they used during their chanting meditations and a newspaper subscription that I could sign up for if I wanted to. I explained that I didn't have enough extra money to pay for those things.

I wasn't asking that they bought them for me—I was just aware that I couldn't pay for it. One of the women who welcomed me into the building told me, "I will buy it for you, pick whichever ones you like the most." They also signed me up for the newsletter subscription for free.

Upon receiving these gifts, I thanked them tearfully. It touched me that these people, who knew nothing about me, were so kind as to decide to give me something from their hearts—with no expectation of receiving anything back from me.

It showed me their character. I graciously accepted the gift fully, and in return, I expressed my appreciation for it. I didn't have money to give back. The woman who gave me the gift also had tears in her eyes as she told me, "You're welcome."

Having the chance to be on the receiving end of someone's selfless gift—being open to receiving and feeling the joy of allowing someone to flow love to me, was just as joyful as when that woman allowed me to give to her. It is mutually beneficial on all ends when pipes are allowed to flow.

It is like the love of a tree that grows more and more fruit, allowing those who need sustenance to eat from it. Perhaps it innately understands the nature of abundance, eternal growth, and that there is always more that can be cultivated. There is no sense of lack or of running out—just the understanding that "More will come when the time is right."

Giving and Receiving

Maybe the tree understands eternity; therefore, it gives freely, abundantly, and selflessly. It does not say, "I gave you an apple yesterday; how dare you ask me for another today." It also never says, "I'll only give you an orange if you bring me back a gift first."

An open pipe allows more love to cultivate, more resources, more giving, *and* more receiving. It is not admirable to cut oneself off from the good things of the world. Starving oneself to fulfill another's own selfish needs (being a giver to a taker) is a learned response to a traumatic childhood, a way to maintain power over another—and so a sneaky way for the subconscious to maintain a sense of safety.

We often do not make changes until we get pushed into a corner where we have no choice *but* to change. Either way, the universe naturally supports this evolvement, and you *will* get pushed to alter or heal what your soul is calling you to transform. Riding with this wave and changing a pattern, even when it is not comfortable, is a way to live a meaningFULL and joyFULL life.

Awareness, acceptance of what is, and an acknowledgment of our learned patterning or behaviors are the beginning of a new life.

CHAPTER 9

Live *Because* You Will Die

Life itself is quite paradoxical—you live, and then you die.

You create a beautiful relationship, then it ends. You build a massive money empire; then it's lost. You live in a beautiful, young, and healthy body, and then you get old (still beautiful, by the way), or you get sick.

These are facts of existence; this is the natural cycle of life—when one form is lost and makes room for a new form to begin. So, if I know that I cannot hold onto a relationship for eternity, why should I even have one? If I know that I cannot keep my money (and it is meaningless once the end of my life approaches), why should I even spend my life working or creating a business?

A Journey into Truth

If a soul knew that it would come into the world and eventually leave it again, why would it choose to go in the first place? If I knew the vacation I was about to go on would end eventually, and I would end up back at home, why not just stay home?

Along my journey that I've shared small pieces of with you, I encountered people from many countries, backgrounds, belief systems, and personalities. Throughout these explorations, I've made it of utmost importance to always think for myself—no matter what another's view of right or wrong, true or untrue, is.

Had I clung to the beliefs of the Buddhists and stopped there—perhaps I would have never been open to meeting all of the other beautiful people that I did. I would never have gotten out of that one limited perspective to come to an even deeper understanding of "truth."

From the moment we are born, we are constantly learning from our environment. Be it from friends and teachers at school, parents, society at large, the country we were born into, or the religion we were surrounded by.

All these facets contribute to the makeup of who a person will become, their views, and how they will respond to adversity or conflict. We learn what words are okay to say and which ones are unacceptable.

In my personal life's experience, I grew up believing that college, a stable career, a beautiful home, and staying at the same job until you retire, was just how life was supposed to go. It wasn't until I was much older that I began to question what *I* wanted.

Would that bring the most fulfillment to me? If I have only a certain amount of time on earth—is that truly the way I would want to live it? Is that a fail-proof route to a happy and fulfilled existence?

Once I became an adult, these deeply ingrained beliefs came crashing right into my face. I was in college, doing everything my family taught me was the "good" path. So why was I unhappy? Why did I feel like I wanted to take a different avenue for myself, and if it were the right path to follow, why did I feel so afraid to take that step?

Choose for Yourself

I didn't decide to leave college until I was around 22 years old. I was terrified to "drop out" of college. As I previously stated, I learned that college was a necessary part of life.

In fifth grade, I can recall my teacher's classroom filled with memorabilia from her days in college. She would explain how important it was to get a college education because it would make us a more competitive-looking prospect for future employers. She was teaching fifth graders to become *already*, focused on making a living.

I never once questioned if it was *my path*. Going to college, becoming "successful," getting married, buying a home, retiring at an old age with a good pension program—this was just apparently how life was supposed to go.

According to everyone around me, college was what would lead to my success in life. Potential jobs would only hire me if I had a diploma (employers wouldn't take me seriously without one).

If I had no job, I'd have no home or cars, and I'd be a "homeless" person with no *worth*. As if being homeless was something to be ashamed of.

Up to the point of deciding to leave college, I was always a great student—I learned new things quickly and got good grades. Just before I chose to leave, it became extremely tedious. More and more, it felt like life wanted me to take a new direction.

Being in college, I felt like I was "going against the grain" of my true purpose in life. Having already had a taste of the shortness of life when I was sixteen, I began to question if it was worth it to stay in school. I was passionate about being a writer, I wanted to write a book about spirituality, and I wanted to help people understand the ideas that I came to know.

From the outside to others who didn't understand, it probably looked like I was obsessed with spirituality. I had a thirst for knowledge that "normal" school did not give me any access to.

In all my years of schooling, I didn't learn ideas about intuition, possibilities of the afterlife, or dealing with grief or death. It never seemed like an essential part of the curriculum to teach students about happiness or emotional well-being, following passions, finding purpose, or living life fully.

These are real-life topics and unavoidable aspects of the human experience. Once I decided to embark on my explorations into educating myself on metaphysics, death, philosophy, and the afterlife, I truly began living my life in the way I believe it was meant to be lived.

My soul did not want to read books about the past, with ideas originating from those who came before me. I wanted to discover the true meaning of existence, and what happens after we die.

I wanted to explore the world and live it NOW to its fullest, not later. I wanted to leave something meaningful behind. I knew my purpose was not just, "go to school, work, pay taxes, retire, die."

I was already deep into my studies of spirituality. It was daunting to take the leap of faith of leaving behind what people told me I should be doing. It would mean diving into an unknown path, where the outcome was being paved out before my eyes. Still, in the back of my mind, I feared looking like a "nobody" in the eyes of another.

Alexis, "the college dropout who never made it," would be tattooed on my forehead—my reputation *forever* tainted (I'm being facetious). Not only that, but once I "came out of the spiritual closet," I knew I could be ostracized by family members who could not understand my beliefs or how I formed them. I would be seen as the "brain-washed" or "weird" one.

Then, there was also the fear of disappointing my parents, who believed that a diploma was the only road to success. I grew up thinking that even if I had to suffer my way to "success," it would all be worth it in the end because there would be a treat once I suffered enough.

But my absolute biggest fear, the most *unthinkable* option to me, was becoming that person who struggled their whole life and gave up on their dreams, to work at a job they despised, because in just ten more years, there would be a rainbow at the end of the storm.

I feared becoming that person who spent their whole life working for another company, biting their tongue, dragging their feet to work each day for 40 years, because one day they'd be able to retire and *finally* start living.

Then they would get there, and there they are, money in hand, and *miserable* for having spent their whole life doing something they hated. They would have spent their entire lives chasing a brighter tomorrow, never delighting in the now. Then they would die, never realizing the true meaning of life. To me, *that* was never an option.

LIVE *BECAUSE* YOU WILL DIE

Understanding that death is inevitable is the reason I went to a spiritual festival alone. It's why I went seeking the truths of existence, got the courage to travel for the first time on a cruise ship (by myself), got on a plane to walk through jungles, and do Ayahuasca. It's the reason I refuse not to follow my passions or dreams.

In my life, there is no yesterday, no tomorrow, just now. I know I will die anyway. I seek to "go into that dark night," having lived whole-heartedly, fully, unabashedly, and courageously.

The point, the purpose, the beauty of my "spiritual journey" was, and is the unfoldment; it's the friends I have and have yet to meet. It's the laughs I've had, the discoveries I've made, the realizations I've uncovered, the places I've seen, the person I have become.

If there were one piece of advice that I could give to all who came across this book—one piece of information I would offer to all who sat before me—I would say, "Always choose for yourself."

Please do not do something solely because your parents taught you that it would be best for you.

If an opportunity arises for you to travel, and others around you are telling you not to do it, but you feel in your heart that you must do it, then please *choose for yourself*.

If you want to be an actor, and your father wants you to be a carpenter, please *choose for yourself*.

A Journey into Truth

If you want to live in a van and travel the world, but someone told you that you needed a big home with plenty of items, please *choose for yourself*.

Someone once told me, when I said I was afraid to love another person because previous love hurt me so much, "Life is not meant for you to eternally sit on the sand, because there are sharks in the sea. Life is meant for you to dive into the water and swim—even if there are sharks."

That is boundless, free, and joyous living. Get in the water. If you fall, you can get back up. If you fail, you can learn. If you get hurt in love, then you can learn how to love even better. If you mess up in an improv scene, a new one is coming. If you have a "horrible" Ayahuasca experience and use that experience to decide never to try it again—you could miss out on a *beautiful* experience.

Wayne Dyer used to tell a story written by Leo Tolstoy about a man named Ivan Ilyich[1]. This was a man who lived his life doing a job he never loved. He fostered shallow relationships and focused on his work, materialism, and his "status" within the eyes of others.

In this story, he develops a terminal ailment, which causes him to face death (head-on).

With the prospect of his life ending, he realizes how futile his life was, how meaningless these objects and his status were. This story inspired Wayne Dyer to not "die with his music still inside of him." He wanted to live his life fully, to give his "gifts" to the world. It inspired him to do what he loved to do, and through that, he inspired crowds of people.

Choose for yourself so that you don't wake up on the last day of your life asking yourself, "Did anything I've ever done mean something? Did I live my life fully and happily? Do I wish there were something I would have had the courage to do?"

One Door Closes for Another to Open

When I was working in Hollywood as a background actress, one of the actors described an audition he had at the beginning of his career. It was a small part for a T.V. show.

He wanted this role so badly and felt so strongly, that he was going to get it.

He didn't get the part. Because of this, he considered giving up on his dreams; that was how discouraged he felt.

As time passed, he continued working toward fulfilling his dreams of becoming a working actor. He continued knocking on doors, no matter how many of them closed. Eventually, a new role came up for the same show, except this time it was the role of one of the main characters. Again, he auditioned, and this time around, he got the part.

Had he gotten the first role, he would have missed the opportunity for this more prominent role. It has been said in many ways (by many inspirational speakers, teachers, leaders, etc.) that a momentarily disappointing situation can become one of the best things to happen to a person.

It is not until they can look back that they can come to an appreciation for what they once cursed. They then realize that the first one, was just not meant for them. It was merely an opening to the right door—a much more satisfying one.

An excellent example of this in my life is when I went to my first college. Right out of high school, I received an acceptance letter to attend a prestigious school. I went for about six weeks of classes. It was my first time being away from home; the college was six hours away. I moved into a college dorm with four other roommates.

I was still experiencing anxiety and depression, so this new environment and being alone, not knowing anyone, was a terrifying experience. You know the feeling you get when you're a small child and lose your mom in the store? You feel clueless, helpless, and exposed to all of the dangers of the world. That is how moving to this college felt.

At the time, I applied to become an animal science major. I wanted to work with animals, in some capacity, maybe become a veterinarian. After six weeks of schooling, I called my mom crying and told her I wanted to come home.

She didn't hesitate. She told me to pack my things. I packed and ended up back at home shortly after. I applied to a college much closer to home and began going there. That was the college where I started my healing path. It was the moment I met that man who made a presentation about music healing and was the moment my life changed.

We can only speculate on plausible outcomes about what *could have* happened had we chosen differently in our lives. I don't think we can know where we would have ended up, had we made different decisions.

I feel that if I had stayed at the prestigious (and expensive) school, I would have felt much more pressure to become a veterinarian or work with animals. I would have felt as though it were a waste to have spent so much money on getting that diploma and not done something with it that it probably would've become like a chain that boxed me into only becoming that.

And again, you would not be reading this book, and I don't know that I would have discovered my true purpose in this life if I didn't close the door on being at that school. I chose a completely different path when I chose to come home. I wouldn't have met the same people at the exact times that I did. If that were the case, all the stories I've told you in this book would be make-believe. Maybe this book wouldn't have ever been written.

In taking the choice to follow each small step that my soul was calling me towards, a meaningful, purposeful, and joyful life, revealed itself to me.

A JOURNEY INTO TRUTH

The Man Who Needed a Cow

On YouTube, I once came across a video of an older woman who speaks calmly, wisely, and peacefully. I came across HaiYing Yang's video[2] when it was recommended to me by the algorithms.

She said that she heard someone tell a story of a man who was once a soldier in a war. He lost a leg and was unable to find a job that would hire him. He became depressed, feeling as though there were "no point to living." He would constantly visit psychiatrists and doctors to find a solution to his sadness.

The efforts of these doctors were ineffective, so they contacted a saint who lived in the village. The saint suggested that they give this depressed man a cow.

He was given this cow, and every day, he had the task of caring for this being. He woke up early in the morning to feed it, clean up after it, and make sure he cleaned its space in the barn.

When it was time, he milked the cow and sold that milk. After that, he would use the manure it produced to begin gardening, which led to him caring for the flowers and vegetables. This became fruitful, so he then had the job of selling the fruits of *that* labor.

As time passed, he realized that his business, purpose, and meaning were the solution to his depression. He could not "find" his sadness anymore because his focus was outside, on what he had to do—not on the mental prison he was in.

Purpose

Someone once asked me the question, "How do you find your purpose?" For many years of my journey, I was trying to figure out the answer to this question.

My answer to him was, "I don't think you have to find your purpose; I think you just have to follow your bliss and follow down the trails that interest or excite you."

I never once had an inkling of where I was going to end up. All I knew was that something lit up inside of me whenever I heard people talk about metaphysics or spirituality.

When I was searching for personal meaning in life, I encountered many beautiful souls. I heard many personal stories from many backgrounds, and I grew a passion for connecting with others. I loved to inspire others when I would tell my own stories of what I lived through.

It just so happens that this path would unknowingly turn into becoming a purpose, something I would want to teach to others. Ten years from now (if I make it there because all that is ever guaranteed is the present moment), I'm sure I will look back on this book and say, "I could never have imagined I'd be standing where

I am now, doing what I'm doing, when I was writing that book."

That is the beauty of life and of embracing the unknown. We have no idea where life will take us or where the storms picking us up will drop us off. We have no idea who our words will inspire, what kind of good we can bring into this world, and whose life we are changing.

Purpose does not have an end goal—it does not say, "I will start this business now so that I will become rich!" It says, "I will begin walking down this path, which my soul is feeling called to walk down, and enjoy what comes my way."

Our purpose develops as a present moment choice to take whatever action we are inspired to take. The action could be something as small as the choice to read whatever book sparks our interest, or to talk to a stranger who could become a future husband. The present moment is where all future manifestations begin. Every small action taken has the potential to lead to much more significant outcomes.

Like I said earlier in the book, I intended to figure out my purpose and what I was supposed to be doing in the world, during my second Ayahuasca ceremony. I wanted a glimpse into the whole future. I wanted to know all the steps to get to where I'm supposed to be.

Remember that quote at the end of the ceremony that I heard? "You don't need to find the next step; the next step will be revealed to you when you are ready."

I want to bring up this specific message again because it leads one to understand a much greater truth about their purpose in life. Many people go searching (myself largely included in this) to find their purpose. They go looking around as if it were lost: "What should I do, who should I be, how can I be of value here, what can I give to the world?"

When I began learning about all things metaphysical, I was also interested in business and personal finance. I would go to writing clubs, learn from and converse with many authors, and work as a background actress. Throughout all of these experiences, I was in the process of learning about more than I ever thought I would have.

I was taking tiny steps to discover the information that interested me. I was following my bliss, my passion, whatever caused me to feel intrigued.

Those experiences were where I discovered my purpose and my passion. I was not trying to become a spiritual teacher. I was in a state of needing help, I found a way out, I began learning how to enjoy my life, and *then* I became passionate about helping others do what I learned how to do. To another, those formative years may seem like time wasted. They were, instead, learnings that were going to become essential at some point down the line.

If you are searching for *your* purpose, passion in life, or reason to live, my suggestion would be to go out and *experience*. Talk to new people, and if you hear about something that intrigues you, follow that trail like a hound-dog sniffing something out. And just maybe, you will "find" what your purpose is.

Maybe you will discover that the purpose of life is:

to enjoy the *whole* journey.

CHAPTER 10

The Truth

So, you probably picked up this book, seeking to find the answers to the secrets of the universe! If you're anything like I was years ago, then perhaps you're asking yourself—what was the mystery you discovered along your journey? Where are the secrets, Alexis?

I want first to tell you a story—and then I will reveal the truths that I've discovered.

There was once a man who grew up being enchanted by stories and teachings of prophets and God.

Because he was fascinated with these subjects, he begins a long "training" to become like these prophets. He begins to think, feel, and act like them, but he still thinks something is missing. He leaves his home and the garden which he tends to, seeking to attain spiritual discovery.

This man has set out on a journey into seclusion, into a desert of emptiness. Step after step, he walks farther and farther away from civilization.

He soon finds himself surrounded by nothing but the desert—this causes him to release any desire to go down any *one* path.

How could he desire to go down a path if there is no such thing as one, out in this desert of nothing?

He continues to wander and eventually comes across a body of water in the earth. There, he runs into two strangers who, like him, also embarked on their own "path to enlightenment" in the desert.

They each bend down to drink the water that is coming out of the earth. One man says, "I have become Jesus." The other says, "I have become Gautama the Buddha." The last man says, "I have become Mohammed the prophet."

The three men spend the night together in the desert, marveling at the sight of the stars. They are filled with awe as they contemplate that this must be what God had come to know. This must be what enlightenment is like.

At the next dawn, the men turn back towards their homes, to embark on a voyage out of the desert. They're heading back to where they began, because they feel like they've reached what they were seeking.

He soon approaches the garden that was his (before his embarkation) and says, "Now I follow the laws of the earth."

He cares for his garden for as long as he is a visitor within this existence. This time, he lives with a new perspective. He tends to this garden, knowing he has lived his adventure, went to understand God, and is now appreciating the simple, the mundane, and the normal. He is no longer seeking what was always with him, even before he took the voyage into the desert. He sees the extraordinary in the ordinary and mundane.

Bert Hellinger told this metaphor within his teachings. I read it in the book *Love's Hidden Symmetry: What Makes Love Work in Relationships*.[1]

I feel that I was that man who went out into the desert in search of deeper "truths." It humorously reminds me of Charles Darwin. It is almost as if I went on a voyage to the Galapagos islands to figure out the theory of evolution. One could say that I searched for the "Theory of the Truth" (the whole truth and nothing but the truth).

I recently said to a friend about my spiritual explorations, "I feel like I went on a big fat journey to try to find the truth, and I finally came to the conclusion that there is no such thing."

He smirked, "Yes, people go on these epic adventures to search for a box, and then they get there, they finally open it, and...."

"There's nothing in the box," I interjected with a laugh.

I discovered that the more I learned—the more perspectives or experiences of "God" I unearthed—the more clueless I became. I realized how little every single one of us knows (and could ever know).

It seemed as if I spent the last six years of my life looking under every single rock that I passed by. I was looking under these rocks to find *the truth*, to find God, to discover the secrets of the universe, to heal myself so that I could wholeheartedly know and share with the world precisely what the WHOLE truth was.

Like a madwoman, I would pick up a rock and think to myself, "Hm, this is a good one, but it's not what I'm looking for." I would then throw it aside and see another rock in the distance, "Maybe that one is it!"

I ignored the beauty of the one "rock" I held in my hand in each present moment. Enjoying the rock that was in my hand, that was the point I missed.

Many go their whole lives, never coming to this realization. How many wealthy people become so consumed with getting somewhere else, trying to fill a hole with money and things, that they miss nurturing the relationships with those who matter most?

THE TRUTH

How many people, like Ivan Ilyich, live their life working to work, afraid to take leaps of faith, never venturing outside of the "cave" to see the opportunities that life could have offered them. That is, had they been brave enough to pave their own pathway?

The only thing that I have learned from my indepth explorations is that you cannot find the truth inside any one book, idea, opinion, meditation, process, coach, crystal, or any other conceptual, physical form.

The form*less* cannot be fully described with forms.

A man told me a story once; it's from a parable that originated in India about blind men and an elephant[2]. He said that every teaching out there is like someone pointing to the elephant's leg and declaring, "This is the elephant!" While another man points to its tail and argues, "No, this is the elephant!"

Yes, they are all parts of the elephant, but they are not the whole elephant. In the parable, each blind man touches a different part of the elephant and concludes that *that* is the entire elephant. Their truth is correct for themselves—but still, it is not the whole truth.

If we are open to listening to all truths to find a greater (and personal) truth, we will have come the closest to knowing "truth." There is no *absolute* truth that supersedes all others in the world. I was in search of that *one*.

I have found it a far more "enlightening" experience to step far away from all "parts" and to examine the whole (with all of its parts included).

I've learned so much more by stepping away from clinging to any one idea—and instead stay open to learning everyone's interpretation of God, spirit, or the afterlife.

What I can tell you, with absolute certainty, is that I have experienced and encountered real-life, personal events that have convinced me of life after death. There is no doubt in my mind that we can tap into that world, even while we are still here in a physical body. I have experienced otherworldly, unexplainable experiences.

I've watched people go on stage and give evidence of loved ones living on in the afterlife. I've experienced psychic phenomena in my awareness and understood its realness by watching it transpire within my own life. I am convinced whole-heartedly, that I will still live on even after my physical body passes.

The **truth** is that there is truth within every truth. It is subjective to one's experience. Like in the allegory of the cave, if I have ventured out of the cave, seen it for myself, and then come back into the cave to guide the others to see my discovery—it is up to those people, to decide if they'd like to see for themselves. It's their choice if they want to eat at my table or find a new table.

I feel that this exploratory phase led me inward, to understand that I do not need these teachers—they have pointed me inwards, into self-empowerment, into a deep understanding (experience) of God that goes above books, concepts, and man-made ideas. Remember the Zen saying I shared at the beginning? "When the student is ready, the teacher will appear."

The second half of that quote is, "When the student is truly ready, the teacher will disappear."

My life has become a moment-to-moment experience of knowing, being, and experiencing God within. Like a scientist deep in research during my exploratory phase, I sat and listened to stories, experiences, beliefs, opinions, debates, and books, meditated in countless ways, tried a myriad of healing modalities, ***all of it***.

Now, you might be thinking, "So you're telling me, you wrote a whole book about truth, to tell me there isn't truth?"

If I *had* to give you lessons that I've learned that contain *parts* of the truth, my list would look like this:

- We will live.
- We will die.
- The mind can be "mastered," no matter where you currently are. Even in the pits of darkness, one can crawl their way out of it one small step at a time.
- Whatever you run from, has the most power over you.
- Nothing is permanent.
- Happiness is more important than success.

A Journey into Truth

- You can make friends wherever you go, never hesitate to travel solo.
- Always dance on dance floors if someone asks you to; in fact, do it even if they don't ask.
- Don't let other people's ropes tie up your wings.
- Forgiveness really will set you free, and it is not always easy.
- Always leave room for growth—in your work, in yourself, in your relationships, in everything.
- Enjoy the steps of the process because there are no ends.
- Make sure you prepare for the worst when you get on a hot air balloon.
- Don't look for bobcats in bushes.
- When you experience storms in life, grow deeper roots.
- There is no such thing as perfection.
- Open-mindedness to new viewpoints will leave room for expansion.
- Trees that bend won't break.
- We don't know what we don't know—and *nobody* can tell you the full truth.
- Death comes with life, youth comes with aging, and love comes with loss.
- You can always learn more no matter how long you have studied something.
- It is possible to turn hardship into something beautiful.
- Cinnamon Bun hugs are fantastic.
- Psychics don't all look into crystal balls (unless they like to).

The Truth

When we are gone, the only thing that matters is that we lived a "good life." The most important virtue is that we lived authentically, left something behind that we were proud of, and became a person we were proud to be.

I have come to discover that growth is inevitable, hardships will happen—and we can become more resilient and changed from them, or let them overtake us, but either way, *nothing* is permanent. This life is what we make it, and it is meant to be lived.

Years ago, I went to a retreat center that had a labyrinth. The facilitators told us we could walk it as a meditation if we chose to do so. They advised that we keep a quiet mind as we walked this labyrinth and that we go into it with an intention.

As I walked along this path, winding from the edges, moving closer and closer to the heart of it, I would smile at and step aside for those whose paths crossed mine. Step after step, I found myself growing curious as to when (and if) I would ever get to the center.

Finally, I found myself standing in the middle, looking over at the paths, winds, twists, and turns that it took for me to get there.

There I stood, thinking about how I questioned if, or when, I would finally get to this center. It became viscerally clear to me how those were the moments that mattered most. Those were the seconds of life that were missed, focused on getting to the middle.

The purpose of life, is not to arrive at the center of any labyrinth. The goal is the journey, the steps it takes to get to that center.

After having this awareness, I made my way back out of this center and onto the same winding path—back out of this labyrinth and into a new way of looking at life.

I hope you look back at your tigers and roar back at them. Well, more like turn around and talk to them, understand them, and love them.

I hope you decide to take the shackles off your feet and begin to make your way out of your own cave, to learn about the reality that I have come to know.

I hope you take a journey out into the desert, live a magnificent path of discovery, have new insights, and delight in the presence of those you meet along the way.

And lastly, I hope you make your way back to the "garden" where you began, with stories of a life lived well, and stories of **your** Journey into Truth.

Epilogue

This book has been a journey to complete, all on its own. When deciding to begin writing and self-publishing, I never could have fathomed how much work would go into it. I have grown so much, just from choosing to take the first step to see this work out to its completion.

The decision to self-publish meant that *I* was the person who decided on the cover design, the formatting, and margins, how it would go out into the public, and to whom.

I researched how to format a book: down to how big margins had to be to account for the space lost in the spine, how big paragraph indentations should be, how big of spacing, what font to use, etc. I created this entire piece with my creative choice, ideas, time, and work.

The list of what I have learned on this self-publishing path, is endless. I researched where to publish it. I found out how to get it into more than one retailer, and how to get it into the hands of you, who are now reading this.

Picture a snail traveling across an entire state; at the beginning, it seems like he will never get there. He chugs along this entire state, moment after moment growing closer and closer to his finish line. He makes it to the middle of the state, looks behind himself at the progress he's made, and thinks to himself, "I've done so much but have so much more to go."

He can't turn back now; he's already halfway there, so he keeps trudging along until finally, one day, he makes it to his destination. That's what this process was like. There were moments I looked back at all that I had already completed, yet I still understood that there was much more to go.

You just read the awareness I came to when walking that labyrinth—that the joy is in the journey and there is no end. A lot of this book has been about enjoying the process—yet still, as I was writing this book, I found myself looking to get to the middle of the labyrinth. How many more steps until I finally finish it and can hold it in my hands?

I find it funny, now at the end of it all, that the cover has a labyrinth, and I can *literally* hold the labyrinth in my hands. Interesting how that works out, huh?

Writing this book was like mining for diamonds and finding one in a cave somewhere. Then once finding it, seeing the potential for its beauty, and beginning to craft it into a masterpiece.

The diamond was the idea. Writing the words, editing, refining, and perfecting, was the chipping away at the imperfections, creating various facets in the diamond to bring out its beauty.

Believing in the potential beauty of the diamond, is vital. This idea reminds me of many of the thoughts inside the book—beauty can be made of something that does not look complete or "pretty" to begin with.

I chipped away about 400 instances of the words "had," "path," and "journey" during the editing process. There are still many instances of those words in this book—so imagine what it looked like before I took those guys out!

I have learned so much about being, or becoming an author, that I'd never have known had I not decided to begin the process. With this in mind, if you have a venture or adventure you've dreamed of going on, take that first step.

Nobody knows everything that they will do for the rest of their lives. Every business venture that ever began, started somewhere—with one snail deciding, "I am going to make it to that state," and then taking the steps to perfect that diamond.

I hope that setting out on this journey of sharing my story, experiences, and thoughts impacts your own life's journey somehow. That was my reason for setting out on this writing venture in the first place.

If you would like to see a documentary-style video, showing the process of me working on this book and publishing it, you can find that on the Vibrate to Create YouTube channel.

As for the future, I'm not too sure where I want to be. I take each day as it comes—live it to its fullest. I do my best to "practice what I preach." Hopefully, I can get this book into as many hands as I can while I'm still alive and begin doing public speaking events.

No one knows what the future has in store for them, but I'm hoping it will be *really good*.

Thank you for joining me on this journey of life!

With love (again),

-Alexis

Notes

INTRODUCTION
1. Murphy, R. (2010). Eat Pray Love. Columbia Pictures.
2. Socrates (469-399 B.C.)

CHAPTER 1
1. (The Dark Knight (film), 2016)

CHAPTER 3
1. Carnazzi, Stefano. "Kintsugi: The Art of Precious Scars." *LifeGate*, 29 Jan. 2016.

CHAPTER 4
1. Watts, Alan. "1.2.3. - Mythology of Hinduism - Pt. 1." *Alan Watts Organization*, 16 Apr. 2019.

CHAPTER 6
1. Phillips, T. (2019). Joker. Warner Bros.
2. Zondervan. (1978). New International Version.
3. Seraaj, Intisar, and Christina Zdanowicz. "Father Forgives and Hugs Man Involved in His Son's Killing." CNN, 8 Nov. 2017.

CHAPTER 7
1. Rumsfeld, Donald. "Defense Department News Briefing." 12 Feb. 2002.

CHAPTER 9
1. Tolstoy, L. (2009). *The death of Ivan Ilyich*. Melville House Publishing.

2. Yang, Haiying. "Unsolicited Advice - How to Turn Life Around." *Www.youtube.com*, 25 Mar. 2021.

CHAPTER 10

1. Hellinger, B., Weber, G., & Beaumont, H. (1998). *Love's Hidden Symmetry: What Makes Love Work in Relationships* (Reprint ed.). Zeig Tucker & Theisen Inc.

Also by the Author

FOR MORE OF ALEXIS' CONTENT:

Want to see footage filmed during the making of this book? Visit the Vibrate to Create YouTube channel for videos and more inspirational teachings.

Find links to books, teachings, and recordings on Instagram at:

@vibratetocreate

Follow us to hear about new books coming out!

Purchase other books by Alexis on Amazon:

- *A Journey into Truth: Unveiling Life's Secrets Companion Journal*
- *The Dreamers Journal pt. I*
- *The Dreamers Journal Pt.2*

Did you enjoy A Journey into Truth: Unveiling Life's Secrets? Let us know your thoughts by leaving a review on Amazon!

WWW.VIBRATETOCREATE.COM
#ajourneyintotruth

About the Author

Author, spiritual teacher, and inspirational speaker, Alexis Gonzalez, was born in Loma Linda, California. Since her first "stages of awakening," at 19 years old, she studied the fields of metaphysics and spirituality, training alongside numerous other spiritual teachers and inspirational speakers. Her teachers include internationally trained psychics, mediums, professional speakers, Reiki masters, and Family Constellation practitioners. Along that journey, she became passionate about teaching others how to find their way through their own life's transformations. She shares her stories, messages, and insights through books, speaking engagements, and her YouTube channel (Vibrate to Create).

The Labyrinth Journey

To be entered to win various prizes—including Vibrate to Create merch and signed book copies (among other prizes)

- Send a photo or video of yourself walking a labyrinth to:
    vibratetocreate@gmail.com
- In the email, use the subject line:
    LABYRINTH GIVEAWAY
- Post your video or photo to Instagram and tag
    @VIBRATETOCREATE
- Use the hashtag: #LABYRINTHJIT
- In your caption, let us know your favorite part of the book or how it impacted you!